The Smart Teens' Guide to Living with Intensity:

*How to Get More
Out of Life and Learning*

D1530785

by Lisa Rivero

Great Potential Press®

The Smart Teens' Guide to Living with Intensity: How to Get More Out of Life and Learning

Edited by: Jennifer Ault
Interior design: The Printed Page
Cover design: Hutchison-Frey

Published by Great Potential Press, Inc.
P.O. Box 5057
Scottsdale, AZ 85261

© 2010 by Lisa Rivero

All rights reserved under International and Pan-American Copyright Conventions. Unless otherwise noted, no part of this book may be reproduced, stored in a retrieval system, or transmitted in any form or by any means—electronic, mechanical, photo-copying, or otherwise—without express written permission of the publisher, except for brief quotations or critical reviews.

Printed and bound in the United States of America using partially recycled paper. Great Potential Press and associated logos are trademarks and/or registered trademarks of Great Potential Press, Inc.

14 13 12 11 10   5 4 3 2 1

At the time of this book's publication, all facts and figures cited are the most current available. All telephone numbers, addresses, and website URLs are accurate and active; all publications, organizations, websites, and other resources exist as described in this book; and all have been verified as of the time this book went to press. The author(s) and Great Potential Press make no warranty or guarantee concerning the information and materials given out by organizations or content found at websites, and we are not responsible for any changes that occur after this book's publication. If you find an error or believe that a resource listed here is not as described, please contact Great Potential Press.

Library of Congress Cataloging-in-Publication Data

Rivero, Lisa.
  The smart teens' guide to living with intensity : how to get more out of life and learning / by Lisa Rivero.
      p. cm. — (Great potential pressr)
  Includes bibliographical references and index.
  ISBN 978-1-935067-00-9
1. Success in adolescence. 2. Self-management (Psychology) for teenagers. [1. Conduct of life.] I. Title.
  BF724.3.S9R48 2010
  155.5—dc22
                    2010003148

Dedication

To all of the young people who continue to teach me daily
how to learn with intensity, especially…

The Writing & Literature Group
(a.k.a. the Wednesday Group, a.k.a. the Shakespeare Home Players),
for your unfailing enthusiasm and generosity

All of the students I've ever taught at MSOE,
for your passion and creativity

And of course, Albert,
for your unbounded curiosity and inspiring integrity

Contents

List of Resources and Sidebar Comments

Introduction

Finally, a book just for you.

I promise that after reading this book, you will never view your education the same way again. *The Smart Teens' Guide to Living with Intensity* is for all teens who care about their education. I wrote it for teens everywhere who feel dissatisfied with the education that they are experiencing and for teens who love learning about things that interest them, even though they don't necessarily love school.

Whether you go to public school, private or parochial school, charter school, or you homeschool, I want to offer you some ways to make learning more enjoyable and creative. I'm excited to show you how to use self-directed learning as one way to live the life you want. If you go to school, the information in this book can help you approach your out-of-school learning in a new way and help you to cope with learning in the classroom better.

Libraries and bookstores are filled with books about learning, achievement, being smart, and giftedness—books for parents or teachers. But what about you, the learner? Where do you fit in? How are you supposed to take responsibility for your education—something adults always tell you to do—when you don't necessarily have the tools or information to do so? In other words, I don't want you just to *survive* as a student; I want you to *thrive* as a learner.

To start, let me tell you a little about me. I am a writer, a teacher, a sometime-public speaker, and a mom. Our son went to a public and then a private school before he decided that he wanted to try homeschooling. Although we didn't initially plan to homeschool for more than a year or two, our son ended up homeschooling from third through twelfth grade. He is now in college. As for me, I am a graduate of public high school, and I attended both private and public universities. I taught for a year at the elementary level and currently teach at an engineering college. When I'm not teaching college students, I work with some amazing teens in an informal weekly literature and writing group, and I have interviewed dozens of young, self-directed learners from all over the country. You will meet a few of these young adults and read their stories and advice in this book. I never cease to find your generation to be bright, hopeful, and as wonderfully complex as the world in which we all live.

Sometimes when I speak to parents at conferences about the benefits of helping their children become self-directed learners, I find myself wishing that their children, especially the teenagers, were in the audience as well. After all, no one can force someone else to be self-directed. Ownership of and responsibility for your education cannot be given to you by someone else; it's a gift that you need to give yourself. It has to come from inside you.

This book grew from that wish to speak directly to you, the teen-age learner. What can you expect from the pages that follow? First, here's what this book will *not* do. It won't:

- ✔ Tell you what to learn when.

- ✔ Give you specific study tips or tell you how to get good grades.

- ✔ Help you to get into the college of your choice.

- ✔ Assume that smart or even super-smart learners should always be high performers or overachievers.

- ✔ Tell you how to homeschool or even that you should homeschool.

- ✔ Give you permission to blame others for what you don't like about your schooling.

You don't need anyone else pressuring you to use your potential, to care more about your grades, or to pad your college application with more activities and classes. I'm not saying that these things aren't important. But I do believe that they are overemphasized to the point of making life sometimes more stressful than it needs to be or, at the other extreme, becoming so much blah, blah, blah that you tune out. If you want to read about how to succeed in school, how to ace standardized tests, or how to write the perfect college application essay to get into Ivy League schools, you can find plenty of those books at your local bookstore.

Here's what this book *will* do:

✔ Help you to understand yourself better as a learner.

✔ Explain how being an intense and creative person affects your learning and your relationships.

✔ Give you permission to set your own goals and expectations while showing you how to collaborate and compromise with the goals and expectations of your parents and teachers.

✔ Show you how to use creativity in your learning on a daily basis.

✔ Support your self-discovery and encourage you to bring your best self to your studies and your life.

✔ Tell you about different ways to teach yourself and give examples of how to take charge of your learning, whether in school or at home.

✔ Assume that your ideal education is unique to your needs, talents, and preferences.

Just as there is no perfect diet for everyone—some people need more or fewer calories, some have to watch their sugar or salt intake, others have allergies, not to mention individual tastes—there is no ideal educational path that anyone else can guarantee will work for you. This is true even if you fit into a distinct category, such as having a learning disability or being a highly gifted learner or having a special talent.

If you have siblings, just think of how different your learning needs probably are, even though you have similar genes and a common environment. I know one family in which one child homeschooled, one went to a public high school, and one went to a private middle school. Three children, three different educational needs, and three different educational approaches.

The good news is that taking more responsibility for your learning will also make your education more enjoyable and even help you to learn better. I remember when our son was learning to drive. At first, I told him where to go, how far to go, every turn he should take: "Go up this way for two blocks. Take the next left. Make a U-turn up here to go back the way we came. See that space up there? See if you can parallel park right there." We would do this for 30 or more minutes at a time in our neighborhood. He was learning some driving skills, but he wasn't having much fun. I couldn't blame him.

Eventually I realized that he would learn better skills and experience more real-life situations if he made his own choices, so I began to ask him just to take me on a journey and to choose the route himself. He sat up straighter and actually started enjoying himself. Finally, when he drove with a specific goal in mind—to return library books or visit a friend or pick up some groceries—he was begging to drive more often. He had a purpose for driving, he felt in control, and he could use his long-range planning as part of his short-term decisions. When he turned left because I told him to turn left, he had little incentive to think about how this particular turn might influence his next move, because he didn't know the next move. If he turned left because he was going to the library, he was better at scanning for oncoming traffic, looking ahead to where he was going, and gauging his speed. He was able to zoom out his focus, see the bigger picture, and be more aware of all the potential traffic situations around him.

Education is very similar. If you feel that you are driving around without a clear goal, if you are practicing skills that don't seem to be leading you anywhere, or if it feels that you are along for the ride but not in control of where you are going, this book can help you to take and—more important—to *feel* responsibility for your education.

When I say "take responsibility for your education," I don't mean that you fire your teachers or parents. Nor do I mean that you are entirely on your own or that there won't be some areas of your learning that are largely decided or influenced by others. Your school will have requirements for graduation. Your parents will have some expectations that might be non-negotiable. If you homeschool, you will need to adhere to state laws concerning curriculum.

Likewise, by encouraging you to take responsibility, I don't mean that you need to be a super student who has his coursework and life mapped out down to the last minute for the next 10 years. In some ways, this kind of hyper-preparation is an example of abrogating your responsibility, not claiming it—instead of giving your responsibility to a school or teachers or parents, you give it to a schedule. When you do that, you remove yourself from the day-to-day choices that you need to make, and you hinder any flexibility that you might need to make a U-turn.

For example, suppose as a high school freshman you decide that you want to go to law school. You decide that to get into the top-ranked law school, you must get into a specific tier of colleges, so you begin now to set up a schedule of classes, homework, part-time work, and volunteerism to fulfill your goals. You fill every month, week, and day with activities designed to improve your college application.

The problem is that law school is still eight years away, and you are at an age when life has many wonderful surprises hidden for you to discover. While planning for the future and working hard are good things to do, you may be denying yourself the free time necessary to pursue passions that arise along the way. For example, what happens if, as a high school junior, you squeeze in the time to try out for the school play and, as a result, fall in love with theater? Will you be able to change your plans or at least reconsider them to make room for this newfound passion? Or even more to the point, what if your schedule doesn't make room for the time to try out for the play in the first place, so that you never learn how much you enjoy being on stage?

Taking responsibility simply means that you know you are in the driver's seat. You think about where you want to go, and you plan one or more ways to get there. Even if you sometimes take a trip based on someone else's GPS route, you know that you have made a decision to do so. You think through your decisions, weigh the consequences, and assume responsibility for the outcomes. There might be many more options for your education than you realized. This book will explain how to find them.

You'll notice that this book is organized in three main parts:

I.   You as a Learner: Interested and Intense
II. Choose to Be a Creative Learner: Divergence and Discipline
III. Becoming a Self-Directed Learner: Teaching Yourself
     and Learning from Others

Part I discusses bright learners through the lens of intensity: intense thinking, intense movement, intense senses, intense imagination, and intense feelings. You will read about how your level of intensity affects your learning and your relationships, and you will learn ways to understand your intensity and recognize it in others. Part II is about you as a creative learner. We will discuss what creativity is, why it is an important part of your education, and how to harness and maximize it. Part III explains the idea of self-directed learning and gives examples of what it looks like, both at home and at school. You'll learn how self-directed learning can help you to make decisions about your education, priorities, college, and beyond. This part also includes a chapter on homeschooling—what is it, how to do it, and how to decide whether it is a good option for you.

Throughout this book, you will meet intense learners like you—some quoted by name and others anonymously—whom I have come to know very well and who have completed detailed, written interviews of their experiences and views on education. They have successfully made the transition from high school to college with their love of learning intact. Their passions range from violin performance and classical languages to wildlife rehabilitation and astronautics. They have found ways in high school to pursue their passions and challenge themselves, and all of them have valuable insight to share about how you, too, can make your education more exciting and enjoyable.

I only hope you enjoy reading this book as much as I enjoyed writing it. Here's to more joyful learning!

Part I

You as a Learner:
Interested and Intense

Chapter 1

Smart, Talented, Intense, Gifted?

I don't consider myself gifted. I consider myself interested.
~19-year-old college senior

What does it mean to be a gifted learner? A gifted student? A gifted person? Does it mean that you're a genius? Just smart? Destined for greatness? That you should be achieving more? That you should be able to skip grades? That you should be good at everything?

Does it mean that you don't need to work as hard as others? That things come easily to you? That you should have no problems with education?

Does being gifted mean that you are odd? Misunderstood? Friendless? A nerd? Stuck up? A snob? Bored with school? Is giftedness something you eventually outgrow, like training wheels or braces?

What if you have never been tested for giftedness? What if you have never been in a gifted program or received high test scores? What if you have always been homeschooled and haven't ever received grades? In other words, like the unheard tree that falls in the forest, does giftedness exist when it doesn't have a label? I would argue that it does.

The word "gifted" brings with it a lot of stereotypes and misinformation. Not everyone likes referring to themselves or even thinking of themselves as gifted. In my work with intense high school students, I've often found this response by Jordan, who began taking college classes part time at age 14, to be typical: "There are perhaps a few things I am gifted at, but I'm not very wedded to the term and certainly don't self-identify as 'gifted' overall."

Labels can sometimes confine us. If we allow them to, they can keep us from exploring new areas of life and ourselves. You might think that if you are gifted, you have to apply to and attend Ivy League schools. Or that you can't or shouldn't enjoy sports or fashion. For some people, thinking of themselves as gifted makes them feel a bit of a fraud—that they aren't really as smart as others think they are. They may think that to be gifted, you need to be gifted in everything.

Labels are easily misunderstood and stereotyped by others. What you or I mean by the term "gifted" might be very different from what someone else understands it to mean. For these and other reasons, many teens identified as gifted students choose not to use the label to define themselves, or at least they don't make a big deal about it. That's okay. On the other hand, some people have no problem identifying themselves as gifted, and that's okay, too. Labels can be useful as a shorthand way to understand a complex set of traits or tendencies. The very fact that you are reading this book—even if you doubt your own giftedness—means that the words "gifted" and "intense" mean something to you or at least resonate with you in some way. The important thing is not what words you use to describe yourself, but how well you understand and accept yourself for who you are.

This part of the book describes what it means to be a gifted learner, but not by using IQ scores. First we are going to look at a list of traits that are associated with giftedness. Then we are going to look at giftedness through the lens of *intensity*. Regardless of whether you think of yourself as smart, talented, or gifted, if you feel that you are in some ways more intense than most other people—more intense in your feelings, your curiosity, your interaction with the world—the following chapters will help you to understand your intensity and how it affects your learning and relationships. If you have been called intense by other people, and not necessarily in a positive way, I want to show you that intensity is actually a wonderful quality—one that can bring you great happiness when you understand and manage it.

Chapter 2

Who Are You, Anyway?

The following questions come from the writings of Annemarie Roeper, an expert in gifted education who believes that "emotions are the heart and soul of giftedness." How many of these traits and behaviors do you recognize in yourself?

Question	Never	Sometimes	All the Time
Do you think of yourself as having sensitive emotions?			
Are your feelings easily hurt?			
Are you comfortable doing more than one thing at a time?			
Do you like to take up lost causes or root for the underdog?			
Are you interested in big questions, like what does life mean? Or what really happens when we die?			
Do you feel driven to understand whatever you have questions about?			
Do you want to know the reasons for rules and where ideas come from?			
Do you wonder what you are meant to do or to be?			

Question	Never	Sometimes	All the Time
Do you think of yourself as naïve? Or do others call you naïve?			
Do you easily see behind false words and faces?			
Does hypocrisy bother you?			
Do you prefer complex ideas and solutions to simple ones?			
Do you tend to come up with unique solutions to problems?			
Does praise make you feel uncomfortable?			
Are you more motivated by your own goals than by outside rewards?			
Do you consider yourself a passionate person?			
Do you like to teach yourself and learn on your own?			
Do you like being precise?			
Do you like to skip around or skip ahead in your learning rather than following a strict sequence?			
Are you bothered by unfairness—to yourself or others?			
Is justice important to you?			
Do you feel that you have strong intuitions about things?			
Do you find that you notice details or truths that others do not see?			
Do you try to manipulate others to get your way, or make bargains to get what you want?			
Do you prefer to make and follow your own plan rather than someone else's?			

Question	Never	Sometimes	All the Time
Do you tend to balk at being taught by someone else?			
Do you like to ask "What if"?			
Do you like words and have a large vocabulary?			
Do you feel a strong attachment to your parent(s)?			
Have you been told that you are unusually responsible for your age?			
Do you feel that you don't want to grow up too soon?			
Do you enjoy friendships with both boys and girls?			
Do your fears take a physical form, such as an upset stomach or shaky hands?			
Do you have a strong and vivid imagination?			
Do you have (or did you have) imaginary friends?			
Do you like to think in symbols and ideas?			

Reprinted and adapted with permission from Annemarie Roeper.

This list isn't a test for giftedness. There isn't a cut-off score that means you are either gifted or not gifted (giftedness is not an either/ or thing, anyway). However, your answers can help you to understand your own traits and reactions a little better. The more "sometimes" and "all the time" answers you have, the more likely that understanding more about giftedness and gifted learning will be useful for you.

Take a look at your answers. Do you see any patterns? Did any of your answers surprise you? Were some of the questions hard to answer because they made you uncomfortable? You'll notice that some of the traits are not necessarily positive. You might have been told by others that you are too sensitive or too uptight, so you might see these traits as problems to be fixed, or you might be reluctant to admit that you exhibit these qualities.

However, all of these traits of giftedness have a positive side. For example, you might not like the fact that you feel fear in a physical way by getting butterflies in your stomach or sweaty or shaky hands. But if you use this self-knowledge to understand your emotions better and how they affect your body, you can learn to manage your mind-body connection and deal with stress before it gets out of control. You can use your sensitivity to your advantage in ways that less sensitive people cannot.

Maybe you know that you can be manipulative (or others have accused you of being so). However, these same skills can help you to be an excellent leader or organizer. The traits and skills are the same, whether used for good or ill. The difference is in how well you understand and direct them.

Chapter 3
Understanding Your Intensities

All of the traits suggested by the questions above can be understood as *intensities*. This idea comes from the work of Kazimierz Dabrowski, a Polish researcher who was both a psychiatrist and a psychologist. Dabrowski found that many people have intensities—he called them *overexcitabilities*—in one or more of five areas, and the brighter the person, the greater the intensities seem to be. These intensities not only affect how life is experienced, but they also contain within them the potential for advanced development and a fulfilling life:

- ✔ Intellect, curiosity, and problem solving (intellectual intensity)
- ✔ Physical movement (psychomotor intensity)
- ✔ Physical sensation (sensual intensity)
- ✔ Imagination (imaginational intensity)
- ✔ Feelings (emotional sensitivity and intensity)

While there are many ways to understand giftedness, I find Dabrowski's theory to be the most useful. After all, if just being smart is all there is to being gifted, then what's the problem? You simply learn faster or more deeply than others and should still fit in smoothly with the rest of the world. Right?

Wrong. We know that being intellectually smart isn't all there is to being gifted. It's the other "stuff"—the intensities—that can cause problems and are important to understand. Ironically, these same intensities are often one's greatest strengths. The editors of the book *Living with Intensity: Understanding the Sensitivity, Excitability, and Emotional Development of Gifted Children, Adolescents, and Adults* describe it this way:

> *[Living with intensity] means that life is experienced in a manner that is deeper, more vivid, and more acutely sensed. This does not just mean that one experiences more curiosity, sensory enjoyment, imagination, and emotion, but also that the experience is of a different kind, having a more complex and more richly textured quality.* (Daniels & Piechowski, p. 9)

As Hamlet would say, "Ay, there's the rub."

The next five chapters look at the five areas of intensity in more detail: how to recognize them, how they affect your learning, and how they affect your relationships. You might identify strongly with one or two of the areas, or you might recognize yourself in all five. Even if you don't think you have any of the intensities, read through all of the descriptions anyway. You could gain insight into a parent, sibling, or friend, and you might learn something new about yourself.

Forms and Expressions of Intensity

An excellent explanation and description of how excitabilities and intensities are experienced by and affect young people is the book *"Mellow Out," They Say. If I Only Could: Intensities and Sensitivities of the Young and Bright* by Michael M. Piechowski. The following list of what intensities mean and look like is adapted and reprinted from *"Mellow Out"* with the author's permission.

Intellectual Intensity

What it means:
- Intensified activity of the mind
- Passion for probing questions and problem solving
- Reflective thought

How it shows itself:

- Curiosity, concentration, capacity for sustained intellectual effort, avid reading, keen observation, detailed visual recall, detailed planning
- Search for truth and understanding, forming new concepts, tenacity in problem solving
- Thinking about thinking, love of theory and analysis, preoccupation with logic, moral thinking, introspection (but without self-judgment), being able to integrate intellectual concepts and intuition, independence of thought (sometimes very critical)

Psychomotor Intensity

What it means:

- Surplus of energy
- Physical expression of emotional tension

How it shows itself:

- Rapid speech, marked excitation, intense physical activity (e.g., fast games and sports), pressure for action (e.g., organizing), marked competitiveness
- Compulsive talking and chattering, impulsive actions, nervous habits (tics, nail biting), workaholism, acting out

Sensual Intensity

What it means:

- Enhanced sensory and aesthetic pleasure
- Sensual expression of emotional tension

How it shows itself:

- Intensified seeing, smelling, tasting, touching, hearing; delight in beautiful objects, sounds of words, music, form, color, balance
- Overeating, sexual overindulgence, buying sprees, wanting to be in the limelight

Imaginational Intensity

What it means:

- Free play of the imagination
- Capacity for living in a world of fantasy

○ Spontaneous imagery as an expression of emotional tension
○ Low tolerance of boredom

How it shows itself:

○ Frequent use of image and metaphor, facility for invention and fantasy, facility for detailed visualization, poetic and dramatic perception, animistic and magical thinking
○ Predilection for magic and fairy tales, creation of private worlds, imaginary companions, dramatization
○ Animistic imagery, mixing truth and fiction, elaborate dreams, illusions
○ Need for novelty and variety

Emotional Intensity

What it means:

○ Feelings and emotions intensified
○ Strong physical reactions to emotions
○ Strong emotional expressions
○ Capacity for strong attachments, deep relationships
○ Clear and well-understood feelings regarding oneself

How it shows itself:

○ Positive feelings, negative feelings, extremes of emotion, complex emotions and feelings, identification with others' feelings, awareness of a whole range of feelings
○ Tense stomach, sinking heart, blushing, flushing, pounding heart, sweaty palms
○ Inhibition (timidity, shyness), enthusiasm, ecstasy, euphoria, pride, strong emotional memory, shame, feelings of unreality, fears and anxieties, feelings of guilt, concern with death, depressive and suicidal moods
○ Strong emotional ties and attachments to persons, living things, places; attachments to animals; difficulty adjusting to new environments; compassion; responsiveness to others; sensitivity in relationships; loneliness
○ Inner dialogue and self-judgment

Chapter 4

Intellectual Intensity

Most people associate giftedness with the intellect—with being "book smart" or good in school. The intellectual intensity that Dabrowski had in mind is not the same as being book smart or being good at school, although intellectually intense people sometimes do excel in the classroom. Doing well in the classroom is a form of intellectual *achievement*. Intellectual *intensity* is an internal drive to understand, a nearly insatiable curiosity about the world, and a love of solving problems that involve complex thinking.

Consider two students in a biology class. One studies diligently and learns the terms easily. He aces the tests but never really engages with the material and doesn't think about the subject except in the context of getting a good grade on his transcript to help his GPA and college applications later. When he closes the book in his hands, the subject is closed in his mind as well. Another student studies the same material but finds herself fascinated by the subject matter. She looks up more information than is necessary for the class and continues to think about what she learned long after she hands in each test.

The first student is book smart. The second student is intellectually intense. One student describes her intellectual intensity this way:

> *My own learning style is very independent and stubborn, in a way. I need to do things in my own way and on my own terms. I have a hard time understanding*

something like a process or how to do something from instructions alone or from seeing someone else do it. I need to try to do it and to figure out how it works on my own. Also, I can remember times when I memorized what I needed to in order to pass a class but retained almost nothing. Then I went back to the text later when the class was finished and actually learned the material. I really have to be into something for it to stick with me. Luckily, I'm into a lot of things. ~Haley

Some people with intellectual intensity are interested in traditional school subjects such as math or history or science. Others are interested in non-school-based subjects such as current events, pop culture, or computer gaming. The focus of interest is different, but the intellectual intensity is the same.

People who have intellectual intensity often love word and number puzzles such as crossword puzzles and Sudoku. Many also enjoy games such as Tetris or other video and computer games that involve problem solving. They find these activities simultaneously stimulating and relaxing. They are usually avid readers. Do you ever find yourself reading anything that you can get your hands on, even cereal boxes or aspirin ingredients? If so, you are probably intellectually intense.

Intellectual Intensity Affects Learning

Intellectual intensity can be an enormous asset in your learning. Being curious about the world and driven to find answers not only can make learning more enjoyable, but it can also help you to remember or retain what you learn. We retain information better when we are self-motivated to learn it rather than doing it to fulfill someone else's request or assignment.

What are you most curious about? What subjects do you learn about on your own, in your free time, when you are browsing the Internet or wandering the library? How does it feel when you are intellectually engaged and really interested in your learning? How might you find ways to feel this way more often?

It's important to know that being intellectually intense does not necessarily mean you will ace every test you take or even have high grades. In fact, you might find that your natural drive to learn and to explore many facets and depths of a subject (one that you enjoy) can get in the way of what other people think you *should* learn to fulfill state requirements or for standardized tests. If this is the case, it is more important than ever that you feel a responsibility for your own learning and know your own goals. Otherwise, you might sabotage yourself in a misguided effort to feel in control. This self-sabotage can take the form of pretending not to care about learning or by rejecting all of your parents' or teachers' expectations, even when they might, in the end, serve your own needs and goals as well.

For example, if you are studying math but are intellectually intense about literature, you can remind yourself that you need not expect to enjoy doing algebra problems in the same way that you enjoy reading Jane Austen. You can save reading the next few chapters of *Pride and Prejudice* for a reward after finishing your math, realizing that learning math is still important for your long-term goal of being well-educated and going to college, where you hope to focus on the study of literature. You stay in control of your decisions, knowing why you are choosing to learn a subject that is not intensely interesting—at least to you—but that is still an important part of your overall plan.

Keep in mind that your intellectual intensity may not necessarily be for subjects that you are best at or that come the most easily to you. You might be a whiz at learning history dates, for instance, but don't feel the same intellectual intensity for history that you do for learning foreign languages, which don't come as naturally for you. When you think about long-term goals and possible careers, remember that your area of intellectual intensity can be what you do for a living or it can also be what you do for a hobby. I think about my brother's intensity in photography. Rather than earn a living as a photographer, he has a day job that allows him to photograph in his free time. This gives him control over what is most important to him and allows him to photograph things that he *wants* to photograph; he doesn't *have* to take photographs to support himself.

If you have strong intellectual intensity and you also are extremely creative or divergent in your thinking (see pages 49-51), you may have trouble sticking to learning tasks or assignments that you did not create for yourself. If this is the case, it helps to know that you are not the only person who struggles with finding a balance between self-directed tasks and fulfilling others' expectations. The solution is often to find a way to feel ownership of those expectations, perhaps by thinking about how the task will benefit you in the long run or by having more control over some aspect of the assignment, such as the time when you study, the environment you study in, or the resources you use. You can also think of ways to bring creativity to what you are doing by asking if you can add your own twist to an assignment or if you can make the assignment more challenging. Don't hesitate to talk to your parents or teachers about ways to help you to be more engaged in what you are learning.

Intellectual Intensity Affects Relationships

When you have intellectual intensity and the people around you do not, you might be tempted to get impatient with what seems like their lack of curiosity. Sometimes others might find you too intense or too "geeky" and make derogatory comments. They may not be able to relate to your interests or keep up with your rapid conversation or train of thought, and you might find their naturally slower thinking frustrating.

You can remember that these frustrations are simply the result of differences between people. People can't help it if they are or are not intellectually intense. If they aren't, they may be intense in other areas, or they might have equally valuable qualities such as kindness or leadership skills. They cannot be forced to be intense or to think intensely if it is not in their nature. Maybe you can't have an in-depth three-hour discussion about British politics with your brother, but the two of you might be able to enjoy playing basketball or talking about music that you both admire.

Rather than get impatient when friends and family can't keep up with your thinking or when they don't find your conversation topics as fascinating as you do, use your energy to find others who *do* share your interests, curiosity, verbal quickness, and love of learning. Look for like-minded learners in local book discussion groups, chess teams, computer gaming clubs, or other special interest groups. You can also look into summer and weekend camps, conferences, and classes, either for special interest areas (for example, computer programming or chess) or for gifted learners.

High school-level gifted programs and classes are often offered through universities, such as Northwestern University's Center for Talent Development in Illinois and Duke University's Talent Identification Program in North Carolina, and at gifted education conferences, such as the annual Supporting Emotional Needs of the Gifted (SENG) conference. A computer search will help you find a lengthy list of these programs. For many teens, such programs and groups are the first time they feel a kinship with other intellectually intense learners, and the friendships they form there span years and geographical distance, as this teen describes: "[I]t was at a SENG conference that I first met people who felt like me, people who seemed to understand me and with whom I connected in a whole new way."[1]

---

1 This quotation is from Joseph Hughes, a 19-year-old whose first novel, *Armorica*, was released in 2010. Read his story about growing up gifted at www.sengifted.org/ articles_social/hughes_through_his_eyes.shtml#jhughesarticle.

Classes, Camps, and Conferences for Intense Learners

The following are just a few of the many opportunities across the nation where you can learn with the intensity you love in the company of like-minded teens.

- ○ Concordia Language Villages (Minnesota)
  www.concordialanguagevillages.org
  World language immersion and new cultural experiences in a summer camp

- ○ Duke University Youth Programs (North Carolina)
  www.learnmore.duke.edu/youth
  Summer academic enrichment in a variety of areas

- ○ Johns Hopkins Center for Talented Youth (Maryland)
  http://cty.jhu.edu
  Online classes, summer programs, and school year courses

- ○ Northwestern University Center for Talent Development (Illinois)
  www.ctd.northwestern.edu
  Summer, Saturday, and online programs

- ○ THINK Summer Institute (Nevada)
  www.davidsongifted.org/think
  An intense, three-week summer program for exceptionally and profoundly gifted youth

- ○ University of Northern Colorado Summer Enrichment Program
  www.unco.edu/cebs/sep
  A summer residential program for gifted, talented, and creative youth

Chapter 5

Psychomotor Intensity

Do you talk, eat, walk, or live at a faster pace than others? Do you wiggle your foot up and down when you talk or read? Do you sometimes feel that you will burst if you can't get up and move, especially when your mind is working on a problem or you are engaged in learning? These are all signs of psychomotor intensity.

Psychomotor simply means muscular activity (motor) that is associated with mental processes (psycho). Just as intellectual intensity is not the same as intellectual achievement, psychomotor intensity is not the same as athletic talent or physical coordination.

If you have psychomotor intensity, you will feel the need to move most strongly when your mental processes are engaged in some way. When you were younger, you might have been termed "a handful," "rambunctious," or a "wiggle worm," especially in school. Ken Robinson, author of *The Element: How Finding Your Passion Changes Everything*, describes this feeling as "needing to move to think."

Psychomotor Intensity Affects Learning

The confines of a classroom are a real challenge for young - children with psychomotor intensity. As you grow older, you become better able to manage your physical self, but you still might have a hard time meeting the expectation to be still while you learn, especially if you are in school.

Here are some ideas for how to make good use of psychomotor intensity in your learning:

✔ Listen to lectures, podcasts, or books on your MP3 player while you walk, do outside chores, or exercise.

✔ Read standing up or sitting on an exercise ball. Ask your teacher if you can read or write while standing, perhaps using a high table or lectern.

✔ Vary where you study and learn. Use different parts of your house or community, such as the library, coffee shop, back yard, or park for study or homework.

✔ If you find yourself zoning out while studying or doing homework, take a break for a few minutes of intense physical activity. This might be what your body needs to relax and focus.

✔ If you enjoy sports, find ways to make them an integral part of your education. If you homeschool and cannot or don't choose to participate in school sports, look for community programs or homeschool leagues to join. Get a group of friends together for a weekly Ultimate Frisbee game, bike ride, or nature walk.

✔ Get plenty of fresh air.

✔ Even if you like to use a keyboard for writing, experiment with writing longhand—cursive or printing. Don't worry about whether anyone can read your handwriting or whether your spelling or grammar is perfect. For some people, the physical act of writing with a pen or pencil on paper opens a flow of thought from their brain to their fingers.

✔ If you have trouble writing ideas that you can talk about easily, consider dictating your papers and typing or writing them later, or experiment with voice recognition software.

People with psychomotor intensity are probably wise to consider careers that don't trap them at desks or in cubicles for hours at a time. Athletics, dance, and theater come immediately to mind, but there are many other careers that allow employees to move as they work—teachers (especially early education teachers), on-site construction engineers, hospital workers, and physical therapists are just a few. This doesn't mean that if you have psychomotor excitability, you can't have a more sedentary job such as researching or writing, but it does mean that you might want to alternate book research with hands-on research, or that you might prefer to write outside or standing up at a drafting board rather than sitting in the same chair all day.

If you know that being able to move will help you think and learn better, don't hesitate to try to explain this to the adults around you. You might find that they understand completely and need to move to think themselves.

Psychomotor Intensity Affects Relationships

Imagine two friends planning a vacation. Juan has psychomotor intensity and is a whirlwind of energy. Alexandra, however, does not have psychomotor intensity; she is a self-described couch potato. Juan wants to spend their vacation water-skiing, learning to scuba dive, rock climbing, or backpacking. Alexandra prefers a weekend of reading at a cozy bed and breakfast, lying on the beach, visiting art museums, or attending symphony concerts.

Juan tells his friend that she is boring and no fun. She tells him that he is pushy and that she is exhausted simply listening to his ideas. These two have very different drives when it comes to the mind-body connection. Rather than berate or try to change each other, they can respect their individual needs and find ways for both to be happy, such as a vacation where Alexandra can lounge on the beach during the day while Juan scuba dives, and they meet up for dinner and a movie in the evening.

If you have psychomotor intensity, others may feel blown away or exhausted by your energy, drive, and excitement. When you begin to feel that you are ready to burst if you don't have a physical outlet, give yourself permission to excuse yourself for a run or a swim or even just to kick a soccer ball. If someone you know has psycho-motor intensity (and you don't), you might be tempted to tell her to calm down, stop fidgeting, or sit still. It helps to understand that this difference is hard-wired—not something that anyone can change. This is the first step toward respecting each other's differences and making room (literally) for psychomotor intensity in your relationship.

Resources to Get You Moving

- *Breathe: Yoga for Teens*
  By Mary Kaye Chryssicas
  Dorling Kindersley, 2007

- Green River Preserve
  www.greenriverpreserve.org
  Summer camp for the bright, curious, and creative that combines learning and exploration

- *Learning Outside the Lines: Two Ivy League Students with Learning Disabilities and ADHD Give You the Tools*
  By Jonathan Mooney & David Cole
  Fireside, 2000
  The authors show how hyperactivity need not be a barrier to academic success.

- "Schools Kill Creativity"
  Online Lecture by Ken Robinson
  Available at ted.com/talks/ken_robinson_says_schools_kill_creativity.html
  Robinson explains what it's like to need "to move to think."

Chapter 6

Sensual Intensity

Are you sensitive to the feel of your clothes or your bed sheets and blankets? Do you appreciate the texture of a really soft cotton sweater, the varying colors of sand, and subtle changes of scent or sound? Does a cacophony of noise make you feel on edge, or do mismatched colors make you cringe? Do certain food smells or textures bother you?

People with sensual intensity derive heightened pleasure and sometimes pain from sensory experiences such as visual stimuli, sounds, smells, tastes, and various tactile sensations. Comfort is more comforting, and discomfort is more uncomfortable. If you have sensual intensity, you probably put more energy than most people into choosing comfortable fabric for clothing, finding comfortable air temperatures, avoiding certain foods, or controlling the amount of noise in your environment.

The gift of sensual intensity is that it allows for a great, even profound appreciation of beauty in all its sensory forms—beautiful artwork, beautiful nature, beautiful language, beautiful music, beautiful scents, beautiful performances of any kind. At the same time, the intense experience of smells, sounds, and sights can often be overwhelming, especially if you don't understand how sensual intensity affects you. Knowing that you can remove yourself from a crowded, noisy party or other congested situation for a while to settle your sensory overload is much better than forcing yourself to mix and mingle when every nerve in your body is screaming for a respite. Giving yourself permission to say no to such parties or crowded events rather than attending out of obligation is probably even better.

Sensual Intensity Affects Learning

If your senses are more highly attuned than average, pay close attention to your usual learning environments. Are you comfortable? What clothes put you in a comfortable learning frame of mind? Does the feel of certain pens or pencils make it easier for you to write, do math, or take notes? Do you prefer to write on a computer or on paper? Any particular type of paper? Yellow legal pads? White unlined notebooks?

Of course, we can't always control the comfort or aesthetics of all aspects of our environments, but there are always *some* things that we can control. I remember being in high school and wearing itchy, wool and acrylic sweaters in winter—they looked nice and were inexpensive. By the end of the day, though, all I could think about was running into my house, tearing those sweaters off my body, and putting on a soft, cotton sweatshirt. My mind was only half—at most—on my schoolwork. The other half was busy thinking of that comfortable sweatshirt. Surprising as it now seems to me, I didn't realize that I could have chosen clothes that felt good as well as clothes that looked nice, and that being comfortable would have allowed me to concentrate better.

Don't underestimate the impact of your environment on your learning—in both negative and positive ways. Begin to notice when and where learning happens most easily for you. Do you need quiet? Do you write better in the morning or evening? Near a window so that you can look outside, or in the corner of a library so as to minimize distractions? Does wearing comfy clothes when you do homework make you more motivated? Or more sleepy? Do you like to have a healthy snack before you sit down to study? Make a list of what aspects of your learning environment you can control and what changes you can make to improve your learning.

Sensual Intensity Affects Relationships

If you are sensually intense, you will want to find ways to let those around you know how you experience your world differently. They probably assume that everyone experiences the world in the same way they do. Unless you tell them otherwise, they will have difficulty interpreting your actions, especially if your primary form of communication is to get irritable or not to communicate at all. It's much better for everyone when a sensually intense person can say, "The noise level in this restaurant is really bothering me. Could we try to find one that's quieter?" Or, "The smells coming up from the manhole are making me feel sick. Can we take another path?"

Don't assume that you should be able to handle stimulations in the same way others do. For example, not until I was an adult did I discover that tight clothing, as well as flickering fluorescent lights, bright sunlight, and loud, sustained noise, all led to migraine headaches. My friends wore tight clothing, sat in the sun for hours, and could listen to music through headphones all evening without any problem. I thought that I should be able to as well.

Even after I realized that controlling my sensual environment was important for my physical comfort, I often had a hard time saying "no" to things that I knew would be unpleasant or painful for me. Would my friends think I was a party pooper if I left a picnic after only an hour so as to avoid too much sun? Would they call me a wimp if I said no to a music concert that I knew would leave my ears ringing and my head pounding for hours afterward?

Eventually I learned that other people usually didn't care much at all if I made choices that parted from the crowd, and even if they did, being in control of my sensual stimulation was much more important than being a people-pleaser.

If you do not have sensual intensity but you are close to people who do, remind yourself that they truly *do* feel many things differently and more intensely than you do. If you can make it easier for them to let you know what is too much for them without making them feel self-conscious or weird, they will be grateful, and you can work to find activities and environments that you both can enjoy comfortably.

Resources to Keep You Comfortable

○ Sensory Comfort Clothing
www.sensorycomfort.com/Clothing.htm
A resource for seam-free socks and organic cotton underwear

○ *The Sensory Team Handbook: A Hands-On Tool to Help Young People Make Sense of Their Senses and Take Charge of Their Sensory Processing* (2nd edition)
By Nancy Mucklow
Michael Grass House, 2009

○ *Wise Highs: How to Thrill, Chill, & Get Away from it all Without Alcohol or Other Drugs*
By Alex J. Packer
Free Spirit Publishing, 2006

Chapter 7

Imaginational Intensity

Do you love to daydream? Are you good at using your imagination to combat boredom? When you were young, did you have an imaginary friend? Did you pretend to be animals? Is it easy for you to act out stories in your mind or to imagine fantastic scenes and characters? Do you often remember your dreams? Are other people sometimes surprised at the complexity and vividness of your dreams?

Imaginational intensity is expected in very young children. If you had an imaginary friend when you were little, for example, your parents and others probably thought this was a good thing—for a while. As soon as you got a bit older, though, you were expected to use your imagination when it was appropriate—in art class, for example, or at recess—but certainly not in the form of an imaginary friend or in any way that interfered with "serious" subjects such as math or science.

The truth is that having an intense imagination in almost any field of study or career, including math and science, is a great asset. In the words of Albert Einstein, "Imagination is more important than knowledge. For while knowledge defines all we currently know and understand, imagination points to all we might yet discover and create." What is sad is that so many of us let this ability atrophy because we don't want to be seen as childish or we simply don't give ourselves the time necessary to daydream and imagine.

Imaginational Intensity Affects Learning

The most important gift that you can give your imaginational intensity is the gift of time. It's very hard to use your imagination well, if at all, when you are sleep-deprived, rushing from one activity to another, preoccupied with the next deadline, or busily setting the world's record for multi-tasking. If you think you just don't have the time to use your imagination, I promise you that if you make the time, you will not only enjoy your learning more, but you will also probably be more productive.

One way to use your creative time is to take a suggestion from the authors of *Living with Intensity*: find a way to record your ideas and flights of imagination. You can do this in a journal, a sketch-book, or a collage. Set aside a few minutes every day to nurture your imaginational intensity by recording your imaginings. I find it useful to email ideas to myself before I turn off the computer for the day. Not only does it keep the ideas safe on a server, but the next day I have the gift of seeing them with fresh eyes.

You can also use your ability to imagine and role play to help you to see possible solutions that others may miss and to work for causes that you believe in. Our imagination is what allows us to dream of what could be instead of what is. Free Spirit Publishing offers a book called *The Teen Guide to Social Action*, by Barbara A. Lewis, that shows you how to use your imaginative power to help make the world a better place. The book is part of Free Spirit's How to Take Action series, which includes titles about global warming, animal protection, homelessness, and other social concerns.

Imaginational Intensity Affects Relationships

Creative writers will often talk about how, when they are in the middle of a novel or other writing project, they live only half in this world. They also live in the fictional world that they have created. They might be talking to their spouse at the breakfast table, but their mind is also having a conversation with their main character, working out the next plot twist, or figuring out exactly what trees are lining the river where their characters live.

When we read about how writers work and think, it sounds delightfully eccentric. However, their family members will tell you that living with a writer is not at all easy. Talking to someone who is only half listening can be very frustrating. It's as though you are sharing your home with a cast of characters that you can't even see but who take up space and time nonetheless!

If you know that you tend at times to live half in this world and half in another, be aware of the effect that this has on other people. This is another reason it is important to create private time for yourself to indulge your imagination. Likewise, when someone you know seems to be on a mental journey to a land far, far away, realize that this is probably not the best time to bring up a new, complex topic or to have a serious problem-solving discussion.

Finally, if you have imaginational intensity, seek out others who share this intensity. An excellent place to start is with local theater clubs and groups. Japanese anime (animation) clubs, computer gaming camps, and writer's workshops are also good places to find imaginative friends.

Resources to Engage Your Imagination

O *Acting for Young Actors*
By Mary Lou Belli & Dinah Lenney
Back Stage Books, 2006

O Cybercamps
www.giantcampus.com/cybercamps
Technology, digital media, and gaming camps throughout the country

O Interlochen Arts Camp (Michigan)
http://camp.interlochen.org
Summer programs for creative writing, dance, general arts, motion picture arts, music, theater arts, and visual arts

O *Sometimes the Magic Works: Lessons from a Writing Life*
By Terry Brooks
Del Rey, 2004

Resources for Understanding Your Emotions

○ *Fighting Invisible Tigers: Stress Management for Teens* (3rd edition)
By Earl Hipp
Free Spirit Publishing, 2008

○ *Mad: How to Deal with Your Anger and Get Respect*
By James J. Crist
Free Spirit Publishing, 2007

○ *"Mellow Out," They Say. If I Only Could: Intensities and Sensitivities of the Young and Bright*
By Michael M. Piechowski
Yunasa Books, 2006

○ SENG Conference Teen Programs
www.sengifted.org/conference_about.shtml
A program for teens of parents who attend the annual SENG (Supporting Emotional Needs of the Gifted) conference

Chapter 8

Emotional Intensity

Do you have strong feelings and attachments for people, places, and even things? Are your feelings stronger than other people's? Do you cry easily? Are you easily embarrassed? Do your emotions seem to change often and swing from one extreme to another? Do you often examine your own feelings and thoughts? Are you hard on yourself? Is it easy for you to sympathize with another's joy or pain? Does that joy or pain sometimes become your joy or pain, even when you don't want it to?

For some people, emotional intensity colors every aspect of their day, from how they feel about school and work to their relationships both with others and with themselves. When they are young, emotional intensity can seem almost overwhelming. If you are emotionally intense, you really do feel not just *more* than other people, but *differently*. This depth and range of feeling can make you self-conscious, feel out of control, or seem at the mercy of the strong, almost palpable emotional vibes of those around you.

Now that you are a bit older, you can start to understand your strong emotions and learn to manage them more. The good news is that emotional intensity is a precious gift that can be the basis of strong loyalties and friendships, the ability to walk in another's shoes, a lasting and comforting understanding of self, and a profound appreciation of art, literature, and music.

Emotional Intensity Affects Learning

You might think that emotions have little to do with how we learn. The reality is that, for many people, emotions have everything to do with how they learn. For example, do you find that you learn better when you like your teacher? What if you feel that the teacher or your parents are angry at you? Does this make it harder for you to concentrate? Do you notice that if you are worried or stressed out about a family or personal situation, it's difficult to concentrate on reading or math homework?

If you are emotionally intense, it is important for you to be aware of and in touch with your emotions so that you know when you need to address or manage them. Otherwise, they can hijack your brain and get in the way of your being able to concentrate.

One of the best ways to notice and identify emotions is by keeping a journal. I use the term "journal" rather loosely because it can be anything from a leather, hand-bound journal that you buy at a fancy bookstore to a pile of index cards that you keep in a box or a document file on your computer. The important thing is that you find a place to describe and try to name what you are feeling. Getting your feelings outside of your head and down on paper will help you settle down, gain perspective, and be ready to concentrate again.

Let's suppose that you are feeling tense and having a hard time studying for an upcoming math test. Take just five minutes before you start to study to describe exactly how you are feeling. You might write something like this:

> *I feel as though I could jump out of my skin. My thoughts are all over the place. I wish Mom would stop bugging me about my grades. Jenny seems mad at me, but I don't know why. My body feels all wrapped in tangled string, and I can't get free. And my stomach is in a knot.*

This quick description helps you to identify several things that are bothering you: your mother's concern about your grades, your relationship with Jenny, and an overall feeling of…well, what would you call it exactly?

This is the next step—identifying your feelings. Here is a list of synonyms from a thesaurus for "tense": agitated, anxious, apprehensive, beside oneself, bundle of nerves, choked, clutched, concerned, edgy, excited, fidgety, fluttery, high-strung, hung up, hyper, in a tizzy, jittery, jumpy, keyed up, moved, moving, nerve-racking, nervous, nervous wreck, on edge, overanxious, overwrought, queasy, restive, restless, shaky, strained, stressful, strung out, uneasy, unnerved, unquiet, up the wall, uptight, white knuckled, wired, worried, worrying, wound up, a wreck. Which ones are closest to how you feel? Write them down. Look at them. Close your journal and put your emotions in a safe place while you study for math. Believe me, it works. It's like being able to put them in an enclosed compartment or box for a while. You can open it when you want to, but until you do, the feelings won't be spilling out into all of the other areas of your life.

If you are like me, this simple exercise goes a long way toward easing tension and aiding concentration—simply by describing and naming feelings. Later, you can take a closer look at what is bothering you and think of ways to address problems when and where you can, such as having a heart-to-heart chat with your mom about how you both feel about your grades, or asking Jenny if she wants to talk about anything.

Emotional Intensity Affects Relationships

Understanding your own and others' emotional intensity is crucial in developing, improving, and maintaining good relationships. It is also an important part of knowing, accepting, and valuing yourself. Self-knowledge, self-acceptance, and self-worth allow you to set boundaries in your relationships with others—boundaries that protect you and indicate that you value your own needs. This, in turn, encourages other people to respect you because you respect yourself.

Suppose you and some friends see a movie that, while artistically interesting and critically acclaimed, is also filled with extremely violent subject matter. During the movie, you feel your muscles tighten. You want to look away. You clench your jaw and have a hard time eating your popcorn. Afterward, everyone else talks excitedly about how great the movie was, either glossing over the violent aspects or praising them.

Unless you understand and accept emotional intensity, you might be tempted to think that your reaction makes you somehow deficient—as in odd or too sensitive. Should you pretend to enjoy the movie as much as your friends did? Should you force yourself to watch similar movies in the future in an attempt to condition yourself out of your reaction, to toughen up? Perhaps you engage in a lot of negative self-talk: "What a sissy I am! Just get over it. Why can't I be like everyone else?" Or you might just stay quiet, not letting others know how much the violence bothered you.

On another day, you and these same friends attend an outdoor concert in the park. You sit on the grass, listen to a local jazz band, and watch the sunset. Suddenly you feel an enormous attachment to the people, art, nature, and world around you. The gratitude and beauty fill you to the brim with good feelings, the only sadness being that you know—from past experience—that you are unable to communicate to your friends the extreme, deep joy that you feel.

People who do not have emotional intensity will not react to everyday life events—both good and bad—as strongly someone who has emotional intensity. This doesn't mean that they don't care or don't feel. Nor does it mean that anything is wrong with you. It's just that people's emotional thermostats are at different settings.

As with all types of intensity, finding others who share your emotional intensity goes a long way toward helping you embrace and value your feelings. If your soul sings when it hears music, you might want to spend more time listening to music. If you are mesmerized by art, you might look into volunteering as a docent at a local art museum. If you enjoy romantic comedies rather than violent action movies, give yourself permission to decline invitations to see violent films, and go see the kinds of movies you like, even if you go by yourself. You might just meet someone there with similar tastes.

Chapter 9

The Care and Feeding
of Intense Parents

Now that you understand more about how intensity might affect your learning and your relationships, take a look at your parents. If you are intense in one or more ways, chances are that your parents are, too, whether they are aware of it or not. Intensity is not something we outgrow, and it tends to run in families.

Does your dad get a hold of an idea and not let go until he sees it through, like a bulldog? Does he insist on doing the Sunday crossword before anyone else has a chance to try? Does your mom spend all of her free time squirreled away with a good book instead of paying attention to you? Do your parents seem more involved than other parents, wanting to understand everything that you are doing and curious about every part of your life? All of these behaviors are less frustrating when you understand that they could be aspects of intellectual intensity.

Maybe one of your parents can't seem to slow down or stop multi-tasking, especially when involved in an important work project (psychomotor intensity). You mom might be bothered by noises that you think aren't loud at all (sensual intensity), or your dad might be preoccupied with every physical ache and pain to the point of hypochondria (imaginational intensity). Do your parents become nostalgic and teary at the thought of your going away to college or getting married someday or having children, even though you haven't even started high school yet (emotional intensity)?

Just knowing that some of the things about your parents that drive you a little crazy are part of their internal intensities can improve your relationship with them. It will help you to understand your parents better, talk to them more effectively, and maybe even be more patient with them. You are lucky to understand your intensities at a relatively young age. Many adults who have always assumed that their intensities were problems and something to hide or be ashamed of do not begin a journey of self-discovery until middle age. If you think that one or both of your parents could benefit from learning more about their own intensities, you could suggest one of these useful books, or give one as a gift:

✔ *Living with Intensity: Understanding the Sensitivity, Excitability, and Emotional Development of Gifted Children, Adolescents, and Adults*, edited by Susan Daniels and Michael M. Piechowski

✔ *The Gifted Adult: A Revolutionary Guide for Liberating Everyday Genius,* by Mary-Elaine Jacobsen

✔ *The Introvert Advantage: How to Thrive in an Extrovert World*, by Marti Olsen Laney

✔ *The Highly Sensitive Person: How to Thrive when the World Overwhelms You,* by Elaine N. Aron

Part II

Choose to Be a Creative Learner: Divergence and Discipline

Chapter 10

What Is Creativity?

Creativity as Divergent Thinking: All Those Uses for a Paper Clip

Get a piece of paper (or your laptop), and in 60 seconds, list all the uses you can think of for a paper clip. Don't edit your list, and don't worry about spelling. If you can get a family member or friend to do this at the same time, even better. Ready? Go.

Now look at your list.

✔ How many total uses did you come up with?

✔ If you were to categorize your ideas, how many categories would you have? For example, using a paper clip to open a letter and using it to open the wrapping on a new music CD would both be in the same category of "using a paper clip to open something."

✔ How much detail did you go into with your ideas? "Bend one end into a heart shape and use the other for an earring post" is more elaborate than "use as an earring."

✔ Finally, were your ideas similar to what others might think of, or were many answers original or even bizarre (such as using a paper clip to make a tiny triangle for a mouse orchestra)?

The more ideas, the more categories, the more elaboration, and the more unusual ideas you had indicate that you are good at divergent thinking. Many tests for creative thinking, such as the Torrance Test of Creative Thinking, assess the following four aspects of divergent thinking as a way to measure creativity:

✔ *Fluency*: the quantity of meaningful and relevant responses
✔ *Flexibility*: the variety of categories of relevant responses
✔ *Originality*: responses which are unusual or unique
✔ *Elaboration*: the amount of detail

Divergent thinking is what we sometimes call "out of the box" thinking. Divergent thinking uses several lines of thought, draws from many areas of interest, and brings ideas together to form new and unusual solutions. An example of divergent thinking in school is writing an essay answer to an open-ended question in which you are asked to draw on class resources and your own experiences to come up with your own theory about a topic.

The counterpart to divergent thinking is convergent thinking, or thinking that focuses on one or just a few lines of thought and seeks a single solution. An example of convergent thinking in school is a multiple-choice or true-and-false exam that has only one right answer and that does not synthesize many kinds of knowledge.

Let's use a driving analogy again. I like to think of divergent thinkers as drivers who are always on the lookout for an exit ramp. They like to travel obscure, dusty roads and follow as many different routes as they can. They would much rather find their own way in uncharted territory—a destination that is a surprise—than follow a map. On the other hand, convergent thinkers stick to what they know works well. If they are on an unknown gravel road, they seek the onramp to the freeway. They keep their focus. They keep the destination in mind, deviating only if absolutely necessary.

Both kinds of thinking are useful for successful creativity. Mihaly Csikszentmihalyi, whom you will meet in the next chapter, reminds us that "divergent thinking is not much use without the ability to tell a good idea from a bad one." In other words, divergent thinking needs convergent thinking to be useful and successful.

While some people are more naturally divergent in their thinking than others, everyone can consciously learn how to be either more divergent or more convergent in their learning.

Challenges for Divergent Thinkers

Much of our education system is designed to reward and maximize convergent thinking. Doing what you are told, following a single line of thought, producing one right answer—accomplishing these tasks well is what schools teach and measure.

If you are a naturally divergent thinker, however—especially if convergent thinking comes less easily—you may have found traditional forms of education to be a challenge, particularly when you were younger. If you are drawn to the unusual answer instead of the "correct" one, you might not score well on tests. If you see novel possibilities in otherwise straightforward questions, you might not finish your work in the time allowed. If you have trouble following step-by-step instructions without embellishment, interpretation, and revision, you probably frustrate more linear, convergent thinkers.

Schools and society sometimes do not accept or even tolerate creative, divergent thinkers who disrupt the status quo and stray from the norm. However, creativity and divergent thinking have the potential to give us inventions of the future, new ways of solving world problems, innovative works of literature and art, and new interpretations of history and philosophy. In fact, in the workplace, businesses often use techniques such as Edward de Bono's lateral thinking exercises or Spencer Johnson's popular book *Who Moved My Cheese? An Amazing Way to Deal with Change in Your Work and in Your Life* to help people to think *more* divergently, especially if their well-honed convergent thinking skills get in the way. Johnson has also written a version of this book for teenagers, *Who Moved My Cheese? for Teens*, that can help young adults benefit from learning divergent thinking skills as well.

If you are a divergent thinker who has always considered your "gift" to be a burden, begin to see the enormous potential inherent in your creativity. The resources listed on pages 85-86 can give you a different, positive perspective on your creative strengths.

A Closer Look at Creativity

One of my favorite college classes to teach is Creative Thinking. We spend the first few weeks talking about what we mean by creativity. Here are some common responses:

- ✔ Creativity is limited to art and music.
- ✔ Creative people are geniuses.
- ✔ Everyone is creative.
- ✔ Only a few people are creative.
- ✔ Creativity can't be taught.
- ✔ Some jobs don't require creativity.
- ✔ Creative people are messy and undisciplined.
- ✔ Creativity and work are two separate things.

How many of these statements do you agree with? Before we look at the many ways to understand and use creativity, take some time to freewrite (see page 54) about your own thoughts on creativity and whether you agree with the above statements. Freewriting is a technique in which you write down your thoughts quickly, without editing or censoring them, to discover what it is that you are truly thinking. Then, we you have finished reading Part II of this book, revisit the above list and your freewriting, and see if your understanding of creativity has changed.

Creativity: Personality, Process, or Product?

Creativity is a complex idea with no agreed upon definition and more questions than answers. Is creativity something we are born with? Is it part of being human? Is it developed over time? Does creative thinking have to lead to a product to be valuable? How do we evaluate creative thought or production? How do we know if we are creative...or not?

Here are three common ways to approach the study of creativity.

Creativity as Personality

This approach to creativity looks at very creative, usually famous people such as Leonardo da Vinci or Albert Einstein and asks what makes them different from others. What does the creative personality look like? What about highly creative people, if anything, is unique?

Creativity as Process

The process approach to creativity is more focused on how creative thinking works. How do we use creativity to solve a mental problem? What exercises can we do to improve our creative thinking, to make it faster or more fluid? The emphasis here is on thinking.

Creativity as Product

Finally, we can approach creativity by asking how to create a new, better, or unique product of some kind. The product approach is important in the business and engineering worlds, as well as in the arts. Just a few examples of creative products are inventions, design improvements, sculptures, musical scores, and computer games.

In the following chapters on creativity, look for examples of each of these three approaches: personality, process, and product. All three can be useful to you as a learner. They also overlap, so I won't break them into distinct sections. For example, the creative personality inevitably leads to insight into the creative process, and much of the time, the process of creative thinking has as its goal a tangible product.

Freewriting

The practice of freewriting is a powerful tool for not only unlocking creative thoughts, but also preventing writer's block. Freewriting is explained here by Peter Elbow, author of *Writing without Teachers*:

> *The most effective way I know to improve your writing is to do freewriting exercises regularly. At least three times a week. They are sometimes called "automatic writing," "babbling," or "jabbering" exercises. The idea is simply to write for ten minutes (later on, perhaps fifteen or twenty). Don't stop for anything. Go quickly without rushing. Never stop to look back, to cross something out, to wonder how to spell something, to wonder what word or thought to use, or to think about what you are doing. If you can't think of a word or a spelling, just use a squiggle or else write "I can't think what to say, I can't think what to say" as many times as you want; or repeat the last word you wrote over and over again; or anything else. The only requirement is that you never stop.* (p. 3)

At various points in this book, I ask you to try freewriting about an idea or in response to a question. When you do this, write on paper or on your computer anything and everything that comes into your head. Don't show the writing to anyone else. Don't judge or censor what you write. The purpose of freewriting is to open the pathway from your mind to your fingers. If you practice freewriting regularly, you train yourself to be more open to your original and divergent ideas without squelching them or dismissing them too early. After all, revision cannot happen until one has a vision to begin with!

Chapter 11
Complexity, Flow, and Creativity

Mihaly Csikszentmihalyi (pronounced "chick-sent-me-high-ee," although one creativity textbook refers to him tongue-in-cheek as "Mr. Smith") has written extensively on creativity and the connection between creativity, complexity, happiness, and what he calls "flow." Two of his best known books are called, simply enough, *Creativity* and *Flow*. A shorter version of his ideas is *Finding Flow: The Psychology of Engagement with Everyday Life*. He also co-wrote a book specifically about teens titled *Talented Teenagers: The Roots of Success and Failure*. His theories have valuable implications for both a more enjoyable, meaningful education and an improved quality of life.

The Complexity of Creativity

In his research, Csikszentmihalyi found that the personalities of highly creative people are more complex than those of less creative people. Highly creative people don't fit neatly into categories, such as being clearly introverted rather than extroverted or objective rather than passionate. They easily switch back and forth between pairs of supposed opposite traits. Csikszentmihalyi (1997) calls these 10 paired traits *dimensions of complexity*. They are:

- ✔ *Energetic and restful*: Creative people can have both sustained bursts of energy and deep periods of rest.

- ✔ *Intelligent and naïve*: Creative people are both extremely smart about some things and surprisingly innocent about others.

✔ *Playful and disciplined*: Creative people have both a zany (divergent) and a straight-forward (convergent) side.

✔ *Fanciful and reality-based*: Creative people have one foot in the clouds and another on the ground.

✔ *Humble and proud*: Creative people are not driven by their egos and may even shy from publicity or recognition, but they also accept and are glad for their gifts and accomplishments.

✔ *Masculine and feminine*: Creative people exhibit traditionally male and female traits, such as assertiveness and tenderness (note that this dimension has nothing to do with sexual preferences).

✔ *Rebellious and conservative:* Creative people sometimes are not afraid to break with the status quo and yet at other times stick with tradition.

✔ *Passionate and objective*: Creative people can fall in love with the world while still seeing that world as it is.

✔ *Suffering and blissful*: Creative people know and feel suffering without losing a sense of joy and wonder.

✔ *Introverted and extroverted*: Creative people are comfortable being by themselves but can also learn and use skills of interdependence.

To understand these dimensions better, let's take the last dimension—introverted and extroverted—as an example. Introversion is a personality trait that makes people comfortable being by themselves. Introverts recharge their mental batteries by being alone or with just a few close friends. They feel most at home in these intimate situations, and they might feel as though they are on stage or adopting a bit of a different persona when they are in a crowd or with people they don't know. They like to think through ideas before sharing them in public.

Extroverts, on the other hand, are comfortable in large groups of people. They recharge their batteries by interacting with other people and socializing. Their personality doesn't change much when they are with people they don't know, but they might get uneasy if they spend too much time alone. They like to process their ideas as they talk about them with others.

For someone who is doing creative work, being able to tap into both of these personality traits is a great asset. Creative thinking requires a certain degree of solitude. Whether you are a researcher or an artist, you need to feel comfortable enough working alone to get the work done. At the same time, all forms of creative endeavor require that the work be shared at some point, whether in a performance setting or with peer feedback. Only someone who has the capacity for both introversion and extroversion will be able to create and successfully share his creations—whether ideas, computer programs, performance, or art—with the world.

Which dimensions of complexity do you already have? Which can you develop more fully? If you know that you are primarily an introvert, for example, you can practice skills of extroversion by being involved in theater, challenging yourself to talk to a stranger at a party, or taking the risk of showing creative work that is important to you to someone you trust. If you are primarily extroverted, you can take a yoga class that helps you to be more comfortable being quiet and alone, challenge yourself to study for a while without the radio or television on, or write about an idea in your journal before talking it through with friends.

Another way that you may be complex is in your learning styles. Whereas many people have one or maybe two learning styles that work best for them most of the time—such as visual learning or auditory learning—many gifted learners thrive when switching between several learning styles, as this 17-year-old describes:

> *I prefer to learn things by reading them, since I feel like I can pick up the basic concepts pretty quickly that way, but then oftentimes I actually have to do problems (in math or science, for instance) in order to understand them fully. I also find that visual aids are helpful, especially when they complement a written description.*

Even if you have been told that you have one specific learning style, experiment with other ways of learning, just to see what happens.

Csikszentmihalyi (1997) suggests these other ways to increase complexity and creativity in your life:

- ✔ Notice something new every day.

- ✔ Do something every day that is not what you would usually do.

- ✔ Follow where your interests lead you.

- ✔ Remember that becoming good at something will make it more fun.

- ✔ Think of ways to make your usual activities more complex.

- ✔ Schedule time to daydream.

- ✔ Be honest with yourself about what you do and don't like about your life.

- ✔ Do what you like more often and what you don't like less often.

- ✔ Don't stop at your first or easiest ideas; push yourself to think of more ideas, different ideas, and unusual ideas.

Flow in Creativity

I am always excited to introduce teenagers and young adults to Csikszentmihalyi's theory of flow. You are bombarded with advice and warnings about grades, transcripts, extracurriculars, volunteer hours, standardized tests, and college applications. In the midst of all this, the message of flow is clear, simple, and refreshing:

Find what you enjoy doing so much that you lose track of time and feel at one with the activity, and do those things more often.

As Csikszentmihalyi reminds us in his book *Creativity*:

Creative persons differ from one another in a variety of ways, but in one respect they are unanimous: They all love what they do. It is not the hope of achieving fame or

> *making money that drives them; rather, it is the oppor-*
> *tunity to do the work that they enjoy doing.* (p. 107)

Many people—both adults and young people—believe, mistakenly, that if something is enjoyable, it can't be of much educational value. I've had parents comment that children seem to be having "too much fun" if they are laughing while doing writing exercises. Even colleges aren't immune from this myth. A class full of students who are smiling and talking is assumed to be goofing off, while one with grim faces and pencils gripped tightly in their hands is thought to be working hard.

This teen, however, offers another perspective:

> *When it comes to anything, especially education, I think*
> *the best course of action is to do what feels right. Don't*
> *force yourself into anything you don't want to do. Keep a*
> *long-term goal in mind, but be ready and willing to*
> *change it if the opportunity presents itself. Get good*
> *grades, but don't freak out over the need to have a 4.0*
> *GPA. Most of all don't let anyone or anything get in the*
> *way of your learning experience. A lot of the time, it's not*
> *what you learn that counts, but the very action of learn-*
> *ing it. As far as I am concerned, if you are going to spend*
> *a quarter of your life in school, you best enjoy it.* ~Casey

Of course, not everything that is fun brings lasting joy or enhances creativity. There is a difference between momentary pleasure, such as having a bowl of your favorite ice cream, and the enjoyment and engagement of flow. For flow to happen, the activity has to have clear goals, immediate feedback on how well you are doing, your complete focus and attention, and the right amount of challenge to keep from you from being either bored or frustrated. When these criteria are in place, you enjoy the activity in a way that takes you out of time. You forget yourself and your surroundings. You automatically work harder to get to the next level, whether in a video game, studying physics, or improving your cross country time. The enjoyment is self-sustaining: you get better, set new goals, get feedback on your progress, lose yourself in the activity, meet the goal, and start all over again.

Overcoming Inertia: Redefine Laziness

You might be thinking to yourself, *All this creativity and flow sounds great, but I'm just too lazy to do what I want to do. I always have been.*

Csikszentmihalyi reminds us that in addition to a drive to create, we humans are driven by a force that is just as strong, if not stronger: *inertia*, the drive to do nothing and conserve our energy. We have another word for it: laziness.

The struggle between the tendency toward inertia and the drive to create is most noticeable when you are first learning a skill or activity. At the beginning, the practice required to learn the basics of playing an instrument, participating in a sport, speaking a foreign language, or learning anything else that has the potential for enjoyment might seem painful in comparison to…well, doing nothing. However, without learning those first piano notes, chords, and scales, you will never have the joy of playing your favorite songs. Without first learning to skate forward at the ice rink, you won't be able eventually to feel the joy of doing spins and jumps.

When you are in an argument with yourself about whether to do the hard or tedious thing that brings later joy or the easy thing that brings only momentary relaxation, pay attention to how you talk to yourself, especially after you have made your decision. If you think of yourself as lazy, you attribute your choice to lack of will power—a personality flaw. On the other hand, if you place your choice in the context of the ongoing human struggle between progress and inertia, you give yourself a fighting chance to make a different choice next time.

How you talk to yourself about what you are or aren't doing can have a great impact on your choices. We all talk to ourselves in our heads, whether we admit it or not. Much of the self-talk is automatic and doesn't even feel in our control. However, we can learn to control more of the internal chatter, and this control can lead to a different set of beliefs about who we are, which in turn leads to choices that support those beliefs.

Here's an example. Suppose you come home from a day of classes or other activities, and although every day you know that you should do some exercise and practice the piano, instead you get online and begin instant messaging with friends. You tell yourself that you will do this for only a few minutes as a way to relax after the busy day, but when your mother calls you for supper an hour and a half later, you are still at the computer.

Your usual self-talk might go something like this: *I'm so lazy! Why can't I be more disciplined? What's wrong me with? I'll never be able to stick to a schedule. Another afternoon wasted.*

The result of all of this self-talk is that you reinforce the idea that you are lazy so that when tomorrow afternoon arrives, you're more likely to *act* lazy. But what if your inner monologue went something like this: *Oops, I let inertia win today. Tomorrow my plan is to not turn on the computer until after supper. I'll write it down now and put the note on my monitor so I'll see it after school. Tomorrow, score one for me!* Yes, it might seem a little silly, but is it any sillier than the negative self-talk you already do?

Never Regret Spending Time on Things You Love

E. Paul Torrance, known as the Father of Creativity, created this Manifesto for young people to guide them toward living more creative lives:

- Don't be afraid to fall in love with something and pursue it with intensity.
- Know, understand, practice, develop, and enjoy your greatest strengths.
- Free yourself from the expectations of others. Free yourself to play your own game.
- Find a great teacher or mentor who will help you.
- Don't waste energy trying to be well-rounded.
- Do what you love and can do well.
- Learn the skills of interdependence.

Share these guidelines with your parents or teachers, and ask them how the Manifesto applies in their own lives. Which of the guidelines do you already practice? Which ones seem scary? Choose one guideline that you would like to follow more often, and freewrite about how you can incorporate the idea into your daily thoughts and actions.

The best advice I can give is not to be afraid to follow your passion. If there is something that really interests you, even if it may fall outside of the realm of normal school subjects, dive right into it. You'll never regret spending your time on things you love, and you'll be surprised at how often even the most esoteric knowledge and skills can come in useful later on. (Even playing video games can teach you a lot about problem-solving, etc....not that I'm suggesting you spend all your time playing video games!)
~Jordan, 17-year-old college freshman honors student

Chapter 12

Sleep Your Way to Creativity

Is your creativity sagging? You might not be getting enough—or the right kind of—sleep. Researchers at the University of California, San Diego School of Medicine have found that creative problem solving is improved by Rapid Eye Movement (REM) sleep. REM sleep is the fifth and final stage of sleep before we wake up. During REM sleep, our brains are excited, we breathe faster, and our major voluntary muscles are paralyzed. It's also when we dream. In a normal sleep cycle of eight hours, we might have five different periods of REM sleep as our body and mind cycle through sleep stages. One hypothesis is that REM sleep allows our brains to synthesize ideas—to make connections between what we already know.

As I was writing this book, many ideas for specific sections (including this one) came to me in the shower. After a night of sleep, I often try to remember my dreams as I get ready for the day. When I step into the shower, my mind is only half awake. As I move into full wakefulness under the hot water, my dream world dissolves in the hot shower mist, and ideas seem to pop out of nowhere. The challenge is to record the thought in my mind, dry myself off, get dressed, and get to my laptop before I forget my shower inspirations.

Most teenagers need about nine hours of sleep to function optimally. Okay, I hear a few of you laughing or sighing, but it's true. I have it on the best authority. If you are getting six to seven or even fewer hours of sleep on a regular basis, you are probably at least a little sleep deprived—including not getting your fair share of REM sleep—which can lead to clumsiness, difficulty waking up, and sleepiness during the day. Lack of REM sleep has also been linked to depression, decreased tolerance to pain, and obesity.[2]

How can you get more REM sleep?

✔ Simply sleep more. Try to sleep in as long as you can in the morning, since sleep cycles lengthen as the night progresses. Whenever you can, wake up without using an alarm.

✔ Avoid eating right before bed. At the same time, be sure to eat enough during the day that you aren't awakened by hunger.

✔ Be sure to exercise every day, even if just for a little while.

✔ Watch your caffeine intake, especially later in the day, and most certainly avoid alcohol and tobacco altogether, which can both severely disrupt sleep.

✔ Try to keep to a consistent bedtime and waking schedule.

✔ Finally, remember your intensities. If your sleep is continually disrupted throughout the night, you might need to adjust the temperature in your room, block out more light from outside, try a different pillow or sheets, or even wear earplugs or an eye mask. If anyone laughs at you or says you are a princess bothered by a pea under your mattress, smile and say, "We creative types need our sleep."

---

2   To learn more about the effects of sleep deprivation, see "Snooze or Lose?", a *New York Magazine* article by Po Bronson (Oct. 7, 2007), available online at http://nymag.com/news/features/38951.

Chapter 13

Creative Discipline: Habits of Mind and Body

We are all aware of the stereotype of the hopelessly disorganized and undisciplined creative genius. His living space is a mess, his clothes don't match, he doesn't follow or care much about rules, he might have one or more addictions that he can't control, and he certainly doesn't waste time making a schedule, much less sticking to one.

Is that really true?

One of the greatest myths about creativity is that discipline and organization are antithetical to creative thought and production. This myth is harmful for two reasons: naturally creative people think that they will somehow lose some of their creativity if they become more disciplined or organized, and naturally organized and disciplined people think that they can't be creative. The result is the loss of valuable (and enjoyable) creative thought and production for everyone. Jane Piirto explains in *Understanding Creativity* that we have more control over our creativity than we might think: "The creative personality can be either developed or thwarted. Creativity takes certain habits of mind. Creativity is not separate from intelligence or artistry, but part of the whole" (p. 37).

We already know the myth. Let's look at the realities.

Reality #1: Self-discipline, organization, and structure are keys to creative work.

It is unfortunate that adults sometimes use the idea of self-discipline as a whip to goad others to change their actions or imply that they should be ashamed if they do not have enough self-discipline. Children are told that they lack self-discipline if they forget their homework. You might be reminded that you will need a boatload of self-discipline to survive in college, the implication being that you don't have it now, and you'd be wise to get it. *How* is not explained. In other words, self-discipline gets a bad rap.

So what do we mean by self-discipline, anyway? One useful definition is this:

> *Self-discipline is the control that we exert over ourselves, the habits we establish, and the choices we make in order to accomplish a certain task or meet a goal, especially when a part of us would rather be doing something else at the moment.*

Self-discipline does not have to feel like a punishment, especially if we keep in mind the task or goal it serves. For example, if you play soccer and have the goal of being a starting player next year, you are practicing self-discipline when you put in extra practice every day, drink more water, feed your body more fruits and vegetables, and do strength and endurance exercises. While these habits and actions are not necessarily easy, you probably enjoy them much of the time. After all, you enjoy playing soccer. When the alarm rings early for you to go to the soccer field for some kicking practice, you might *at the moment* wish you could stay in bed, but once you are out there in the morning air, feeling the ball against your cleats, you know that you are working toward a longer-lasting happiness and greater joy than an extra 30 minutes of sleep would bring.

Self-discipline is a key to creative work because it allows you to gain control of your environment and schedule, freeing both space and time for creativity. For example, suppose you love to write and would like to write more, although you don't have more specific goals in mind. You know that you're creative, and you think about your writing a lot. However, you aren't very organized with your writing or your schoolwork. Whenever an assignment is due for a class, you spend at least half an hour looking for the assignment sheet before you can start. Even more frustrating, you procrastinate. Every morning you wake up with big ideas for what you would like to write, but the day soon becomes filled simply trying to meet other deadlines for which you have not planned ahead. The result is that not only do you never have time to write, you feel bad about yourself for not meeting your creative goals.

Now let's look at how self-discipline—organizing yourself, your space, and your time—could help.

To organize yourself, you would write down your priorities. They wouldn't be floating around in your head without anything to anchor them. You put them on paper, even if you are the only one to ever see them and even if you change them later. You write specific goals that you want to meet, such as writing a short story every two months or finishing a novel in a year, rather than a vague idea of "writing more" or "writing better." In addition to these larger goals, you would plan smaller steps to get you there, such as writing for a certain amount of time or a specific number of words each day. Finally, you would control your thoughts so as not to beat yourself up when you miss a step or two. You would have compassion with yourself—something that also takes self-discipline.

To organize your space, you would find a system of filing or piling that works for you. Some people like to use colorful file folders or shelves and three-ring binders. Others organize in a more free-form way, with loose piles and boxes. As long as you know where things are and can find them when you need them, any organization system will do. This allows you to avoid wasting time looking through everything on the floor for what you need (and we all know that the mess we make looking frantically for that one piece of paper results in even more lost time later). Your sorted files or piles would also give you a visual reminder of what needs to be done, what project is already finished, and what is important to you. This, in turn, adds to your self-esteem and your motivation to do well.

To organize your time, you must first be aware of the passage of time. You spend a little time each morning and evening thinking about your day. Rather than have time rush past you like a waterfall or drip past like a leaky faucet, you get in your rowboat and work with time, using its currents and flow to help you to get where you want to go. For some people, using time well means writing down an hour-by-hour schedule, checking off items on a to-do list, or using an electronic organizer. For others, it just means having a flexible but very clear idea of how your day will progress, what you will do when, and how you will handle inevitable interruptions and last-minute changes.

What are the results of all of this self-discipline and organization? You now know and have recorded what you want to accomplish with your creative writing, so when you sit down to write, you don't waste time staring at a blank paper or screen. You are on top of other tasks and assignments, so when you have time scheduled to write, you can write, not play catch-up with procrastination. Finally, and perhaps most important, your mind is clearer, freer to make connections and to have new ideas. By organizing the world around you, you can put that world out of your mind for the time being, leaving you free to create. At the same time, you give your ego a boost and make it more likely that you will live the life you want rather than just get through the day. Mary-Elaine Jacobsen, author of *The Gifted Adult*, puts it this way:

> *The difference between the creative person and the creative producer is hard work. Those who actually produce the play, build the rocket, find the cure, and write the novel don't let their ideas collect dust on the "tomorrow" shelf. They dig in, often before they feel completely ready, and keep digging until they unearth what they are searching for.* (p. 158)

Reality #2: Self-discipline, organization, and scheduling are skills that can be practiced and strengthened, not traits that some people have and others don't.

For many years, I was convinced that I could never learn to be organized—that I just wasn't someone who knew how to "dig in." I couldn't seem to stick to a schedule. I certainly lacked the self-discipline skills to work systematically and with persistence toward important goals. Most of the time, I thought of myself as lazy.

On the outside, I don't think that these self-doubts were obvious to others. I kept up with my schoolwork and did well; in fact, I was class valedictorian. I was involved in a lot of activities, from band and theater to student government and the school newspaper. While I often finished tasks and assignments just in the nick of time, I did meet my deadlines—barely.

None of that really mattered, though, because on the inside, I didn't feel good about anything I accomplished. I felt that I was just lucky and a bit of a fraud, and I knew that I wasn't working toward goals that mattered to me. I got good grades because…well, because I was expected to and schoolwork was easy for me, not because I consciously worked for them. I was involved in all of those activities because everyone else was, and again, it's what was expected for college applications. I spread my time around doing so many different things that I didn't have a clear sense of my priorities. I didn't even know which activities I enjoyed and which ones I didn't. At the same time, I mistakenly thought that my inability to plan my life was somehow the price I had to pay for my love of all things creative.

Does this sound familiar? If so, I have good news. You can change. If I did it, anyone can! I didn't change my core personality, my tendency toward divergent thinking, or my love of creative activities and open-ended questions. What I did change were my thought processes and my habits. In recent years, for the first time in my life, I have begun experiencing the joy of being organized. That's right, *joy*. I confess that I will probably never have an orderly life like that of the people who are organization experts. However, I have learned to break big tasks and goals into small steps, to congratulate myself for whatever steps I do take, to make lists, to meet deadlines, and to take control of my time. And I can tell you that it makes life a whole lot more fun.

So if you think that organization and self-discipline are for those lucky few who are born that way, here are some ways to start claiming those skills for yourself:

✔ *Think small.* Start with baby steps rather than giant leaps. Take your room, for example. If you decide that you will organize it in one fell swoop, you'll probably start with energy and enthusiasm, but after an hour or two, you'll stand exhausted in a more confusing and disheartening disarray than you had to start with. It's much better to give yourself even more time than you think you'll need and break the task into the smallest of steps. For example, spend just five minutes each day for the next month cleaning a square foot—more or less—of your room, whether that space be a bookshelf, on the floor, or a desk drawer. In a month, not only will you have a much neater living space, but you will have built the habit of daily de-cluttering.

✔ *Dream big.* Set aside an hour every week to think about your goals. Better yet, use freewriting (see page 54) as a way to help your thinking. Make a list of everything you want to do—this week, this month, this year, or this lifetime. Then look at the list and circle the things that are most important to you and cross out the things that aren't. Transfer the circled goals to another piece of paper, and start listing all the ways you can think of to get there. Whether your ultimate goals are modest or monumental, think small as you chart your path to reach them. Do you want to learn to play "Maple Leaf Rag" on the piano? Make your first baby step to learn the first five measures. Do you want to major in foreign languages in college so that you can become an ambassador? Make your first baby step to research all of the ways available to begin learning Japanese. This planning time should be unhurried, fun, and a gift you give yourself. Allow yourself to dream big and plan small.

✔ *Put your goals and plans in writing.* You might want to keep a journal in which you record all of your plans. Or maybe you prefer to use an electronic organizer or a school planner. Other ideas include a large whiteboard in your room with colored markers or a sketchbook for drawings as well as writing. Whatever you do, don't rely on keeping all of your ideas and plans in your head. I once heard someone at a conference say that planning isn't thinking—planning is writing.

✔ *Be kind to and patient with yourself when you falter.* Let's put it out there at the beginning: you will sometimes not follow your plan. You will be imperfect. You are human. Life is messy. What usually happens when we fail to follow a plan? We throw our hands up in frustration and give up. If we can't do it perfectly, we won't do it at all! We berate ourselves for having "failed." If we're really good at berating ourselves, we'll add "yet again." However, what would you say to a good friend who failed to follow his schedule for a day? You'd probably tell him not to be hard on himself and to get back on track tomorrow. "You can do it! Don't dwell on what's already done." Get in the habit of saying the same things to yourself. While it's true that we can be our own worst critics, it's also true that we can be our own best cheerleaders.

✔ *Celebrate successes, big and small.* When you meet a goal, whether it is running a 5K race or finishing a math assignment the day before it's due, find a way to congratulate yourself. The easiest way is to use your thoughts. Take a moment to tell yourself, "Good work!" "You're doing it." "Way to go." There is no need to feel self-conscious because no one can hear you. Like anything else, thinking positive thoughts about yourself is a habit that is hard to develop at first but gets easier and more automatic with time. Other ways to celebrate success are to treat yourself to a movie, a new book, or some favorite music. Whatever you do, don't allow even small successes to go unnoticed or unrecognized. By taking the time to notice them, you boost your confidence and begin to think of yourself as someone who has self-discipline, which becomes a self-fulfilling belief.

Reality #3: Bright, gifted people may have to think more consciously about self-discipline because so much comes easily to them.

If learning tasks have always come easily to you, you probably had little incentive as a child to learn skills of time management or organization. This is one reason why programs for gifted students focus on providing challenge at a higher or deeper level. Of course, if the work is too difficult, you become frustrated. But if it's too easy, your self-discipline skills aren't used enough to get stronger.

For example, if you have a paper due in a week and you know that you can write it the night before and still get the highest grade possible (or get feedback from your parents indicating that you did as well as you were expected to do), why motivate yourself to work on it ahead of time? However, by doing last-minute work, you don't learn to write successive drafts, to revise, or to get feedback from others before editing your own work—all important skills for any serious writer.

Doing just enough to get by can become a trap for gifted students. At the time, it seems as though you are making things easy for yourself. But many gifted teens get to college and find themselves having to handle a workload that they don't have the organizational skills to manage. Their grades are lower than they are used to, and they begin to question whether they were ever very bright to begin with as they find themselves learning alongside peers who, because learning did *not* come as easily for them, long ago established good study habits and time management skills.

What can you do? First, remember that your education is your own. You can develop the necessary study and organizational skills if you are struggling. Or, if you are in a class that is not challenging, you can take responsibility to rev up the challenge to the point of your needing to work to learn. Remember that the right level of challenge will make it more likely that you will find flow and enjoyment in your work. You are doing this for you, not for anyone else. You might be able to talk to the teacher about adjusting the assignments. Or you can do some more in-depth study on your own of topics that are of interest to you. As a self-directed learner—which we'll learn more about later—what you don't have is the option of blaming others or shrugging your shoulders with a "What can I do?" attitude.

If you know that your self-discipline muscles could use a workout, begin to use them in small ways on a regular basis. Before you go to bed, get everything ready for the next day—clothes, books, workout gear—and use the time you save in the morning to listen to some favorite music or read from an interesting book to start your day. The next time you are tempted to grab the remote control and plop on the couch when it's time for guitar practice, remind yourself that the time spent learning new chords leads to skills that can bring future joy, whereas watching another rerun is over as soon as you turn off the television set. The secret is not to deny yourself for the sake of denying yourself, but to choose one activity over another because it will make you happier (which is different from bringing momentary pleasure or inertia). As this teen explains, doing hard work before easy work is also a good habit to develop:

> *I like to be able to set my own schedule. I prefer to work on the harder material earlier in the week, and usually earlier in the day as well, since that is when I have the most energy. I've found that I tend to work better doing a little bit every day rather than working in large clumps less regularly, but sometimes the temptation to focus on one topic that interests me is too great.* ~Jordan

Gaining skills of self-discipline is no different from starting a physical exercise program, taking up a new sport, or learning a musical instrument. You don't begin by bench pressing one hundred pounds, playing golf against the local pro, or trying to play a Chopin etude. You begin with five-pound weights, putting practice, or finger exercises and scales. You do it not to punish yourself or because anyone else thinks you should; you do it to live the life you want.

Chapter 14

Waiting until the Last Minute: Procrastination, Perfectionism, and Creativity

Who among us doesn't procrastinate at least once in a while? Only robots always do proper tasks in the proper order at the proper time. Unlike robots, human beings are occasionally distracted, have unexpected ideas, shift our priorities at the last minute, or simply go on a mini-strike, especially when we feel overwhelmed or when we lack a clear direction.

For some people, however, procrastination becomes a way of life. When procrastination becomes habitual, it can get in the way of not only short-term accomplishment, but long-term happiness and peace of mind. If we procrastinate long enough, we eventually find ourselves buried under a pile of missed deadlines and failed responsibilities. When this happens, we wake up each morning dreading yet another day of trying to catch up with yesterday's (or last week's or last month's) to-do list. As the psychologist William James reminds us, procrastination is exhausting: "Nothing is so fatiguing as the eternal hanging on of an uncompleted task."

Here's the good news: procrastination need not define nor rule you. By managing your tendency to procrastinate, you can make room for more creativity in your life and add more energy to your days. Before we look at how to take charge of procrastination and how not putting off until tomorrow can reap benefits today, let's look at why we procrastinate in the first place.

Why We Procrastinate

Here are four common reasons for waiting until the last minute to do what we know we should be doing:

- ✔ Perfectionism
- ✔ Lack of goals or planning
- ✔ Lack of interest or investment
- ✔ Too much (or too little) to do

Perfectionism

When you think of a perfectionist, what comes to mind? The straight-A student who never makes a mistake, never hands in a late paper, and never gets into trouble? Someone who never misspells a word and whose handwriting is as neat as computer type? Someone who panics at the thought of an A-minus or a lost assignment?

Not necessarily.

While some perfectionists do fit this description, many others appear on the outside to not care much at all about being perfect. Parents and teachers might refer to them as underachievers or non-achievers. These students hand in papers typed the night before, if at all. They scoff at the expectations that others think they should have. Rather than accomplish too much, they seem to accomplish little at all. How could they be perfectionists?

Perfectionism has more to do with what goes on in our heads than what our lives look like on the outside. Perfectionism is all about what Mary-Elaine Jacobsen, author of *The Gifted Adult*, calls an "urge to perfect." People with an urge to perfect want things to be "just so." They notice slight changes in their environment or their work and are driven to seek a better way, a better solution, a better result.

When we haven't learned to understand and manage this urge to perfect, we might go to one of two extremes. We can become the anxiety-ridden overachiever described above, or we might just decide that rather than risk the pain of not measuring up to our own or others' standards, we won't try at all. We procrastinate because if, in the end, we don't do as well as we want, we have an excuse. If we get a "C" on a test that we didn't study for, we can blame it on not giving it our all, or we can congratulate ourselves on doing as well as we did, considering we didn't try. But if we get a "C" on a test that we thought we were prepared for, we must deal with the intense discomfort that we feel with not being perfect.

In addition, many people mistakenly think that being gifted means doing well without trying—in short, if you do well because you work hard, you must not be gifted. This faulty reasoning probably began when you were young, maybe even before you can remember, when others praised learning skills—reading, writing, math—that came easily to you or that you did at a younger age than usual. Of course, you were just learning according to your own timetable, and it probably didn't seem very difficult at all, but the message was that being smart or gifted was mainly about accomplishment or learning that seems effortless.

Think about the last time you put off doing something that was important. Is it possible that you were fearful of not doing as well as you (or others) expected? Could procrastination have been your way of giving yourself an excuse if the result wasn't up to par? Or could your expectations for yourself be so impossibly high that you know it's pointless even to begin?

Lack of Goals or Planning

Even if we have reasonable expectations and understand our urge to perfect, we might procrastinate because we simply don't know where to begin. Either we don't have a clear idea of our long-term goal, or we don't have a detailed enough plan of how to get there.

For example, suppose you have an essay due in a week. You sit down to begin, only to stare for several minutes at your computer screen. No ideas arrive, so you open another tab and check your email, then you browse your favorite movie review site. You remember your essay and tell yourself that you really must focus. Still no ideas come. Finally you give up and tell yourself that you have an entire week, so you will try again tomorrow. Tomorrow comes, and you go through the routine all over again.

What's going on here? Clearly you aren't putting off the work entirely or pretending that the assignment doesn't exist. The problem is that you literally don't know where to start. The goal of "write an essay" is too vague by itself, and you haven't broken the task into smaller, more manageable steps. It's as if someone told you to take a road trip across the country but forgot to give you a map or a compass or even a specific destination.

You might think that some people are just good at planning and others aren't. I used to think that way, too. The truth is that learning to set small goals so as to meet larger ambitions is a skill that improves with practice. Often, the first step is simply realizing that planning takes a little time at the beginning of a project—time that will pay off in big ways later on. We might be tempted to jump right into a new idea while our excitement is high, but we can use that excitement instead to think through the details of our idea and set small goals that will improve our chances of success without running out of gas later due to lack of foresight.

Consider Julie in the book and movie *Julie & Julia*. Instead of plunging into her blog with the vague goal of writing about cooking, Julie's chances of success increased as her goal became more specific—to work her way through all of the 524 recipes in Julia Child's *Mastering the Art of French Cooking* in 365 days, and write daily about her experiences. By taking the time to set similar goals for ourselves, we wake up each day knowing exactly what small steps we need to take without the worry of where we are going or how we will get there.

What if you are not in the habit of planning—if it feels awkward or frustrating? You can spend some time observing the "natural planners" around you and take note of their techniques. And eye-opener for me was visiting my family one year for Thanksgiving and watching my step-mother—someone I had always considered a natural planner—take the time to keep a holiday to-do list on a piece of scratch paper, crossing off items as they were finished and adding new ones as they arose. That's when I realized that the household organization and entertaining that she made look so easy was the result of setting and keeping track of small goals, one at a time, and that maybe I could learn to do so as well.

Lack of Interest or Investment

What if you know how you should begin and what your expectations are, but you still find yourself putting off until tomorrow what should be done today? Maybe the task or project is just not that important to you, or you don't feel an investment in what you are doing.

Review the idea of flow on page 58. Is it possible that you are procrastinating because you aren't remembering the long-term satisfaction that awaits you in the future? You might not be interested in doing the algebra review problems today, but you know that you are definitely interested in becoming a mechanical engineer in the future. In this case, it's not that you aren't interested or passionate about the larger goal; you just have forgotten to connect the dots between short-term work and long-term joy.

Alternatively, is it possible that you are involved in an activity whose time has come to an end? If you find yourself chronically late for gymnastics practice, for example, and "forgetting" to stretch or practice flips, perhaps you would rather be doing something else. Not all interests and pursuits last forever, and there is nothing wrong with, after careful thought and review, letting one activity come to its natural end so that you can begin something else anew.

Finally, are you going through the motions rather than investing yourself in what you are supposed to be doing? Investing ourselves means allowing ourselves—mind and body—to care about and to give our full attention to whatever we are doing at the moment. The next time you find yourself procrastinating, stop for a moment to check if your thoughts are really somewhere else and whether gently bringing them back to whatever is in front of you helps you to stay on task and finish the job.

Too Much (Or Too Little) to Do

Finally, a common reason for procrastination is being over-scheduled. When we are trying to do too much, our bodies and minds scream for a rest, and we often unconsciously put off necessary work precisely when we have the most to do just to give ourselves a break. When we have too much to do, however, even a small break means that we fall behind, and the more behind we get, the more stressed we feel and the more breaks we feel we need.

Doing too much is easier today than ever before. There is pressure from adults to build up your college résumé. Advances in technology and transportation make it easier to participate in interest groups and sports and online social groups. Many high schools routinely assign several hours of homework a night, especially for AP and honors courses. When all of this becomes too much, some students rebel—either consciously or unconsciously—by procrastinating. The short-term gratification of inertia becomes too strong.

Miriam Adderholdt and Jan Goldberg, authors of *Perfectionism: What's Bad about Being Too Good*, suggest that choosing to do too much can also be related to perfectionism. If we pack our lives full enough, we never have to worry about not meeting our high expectations because we can always say, "I would have done better if I weren't so busy or had more time." In this way, overscheduling is really a form of self-sabotage that also allows us to complain—with just a touch of self-righteousness—about being "too busy."

For some people, procrastination pays a visit when they are underscheduled rather than overscheduled. It's common for people to look forward to vacation time or summers when they can finally do all of the things that they have wanted to do, only to find that those days and weeks slip through their fingers without them accomplishing any of their goals. The momentum of a comfortably busy day keeps us going, both physically and mentally, and for some people, lack of structure and activity leads only to more lack of structure and activity. If this sounds familiar, remember Mihaly Csikszentmihalyi's idea of the power of inertia and the drive to do nothing.

Managing Procrastination

Now that you have some ideas as to why you might procrastinate, let's look at ways to make procrastination an occasional rather than a habitual part of your life, as well as how managing procrastination can enhance your creativity.

Embrace Your Urge to Perfect

Regardless of what others might tell you, being a perfectionist is not a character flaw! Wanting to do the best work possible, being an idealist, taking care with details—these are all noble and worthy traits. The urge to perfect was what drove Rembrandt to paint portraits that seem to be alive. It's what motivated Edison to explore more than 2,000 theories before he invented what we know now as the lightbulb. It's what helped Martin Luther King, Jr. to practice speeches in front of a mirror until he was satisfied, gymnast Shawn Johnson to train four hours a day to prepare for the 2008 Olympics, and J.K. Rowling to rewrite one chapter of the fourth Harry Potter book 13 times until it was "just so."

In fact, the urge to perfect can be a source of joy. Have you ever felt a thrill after doing something perfectly or nearly perfectly, whether in sports or video games or schoolwork? That thrill comes from an inner urge to perfect that has been satisfied. Don't be ashamed of your urge to perfect. It is part of who you are.

Remember that Imperfection Is Necessary for Creativity

Ken Robinson, author of *The Element: How Finding Your Passion Changes Everything*, reminds us that to be creative, we must "be willing to be wrong." If we live a life whose main purpose is to avoid mistakes, imperfection, and messiness, we sacrifice creativity.

Part of the creative process is trying out new ideas and sifting through those ideas to find the best ones. However, if we limit ourselves to only one or two ideas to start with—the "perfect" ones or the only ones that we have time for because we procrastinated too long—we simply don't have enough creative material—mistakes and all—to choose from. Trying too hard to be perfect gets in the way of doing our best.

Let's return to our example of writing an essay. If you wait until the last minute, you will have very few choices of what to submit because of lack of time. However, if you start ahead of time, knowing that your first drafts will not be very good, you will have the time you need to try ideas and discard them, build on false starts, and polish rough edges. You have to be willing to be wrong, to write a terrible first draft, in order to produce a fantastic final draft.

Even after you find a right answer or a good idea, don't stop there. Dewitt Jones, a *National Geographic* photographer, says that the key to creativity is to know that "there is more than one right answer." Creative people give themselves the time to come up with several good or right answers or products. This allows them to build on their success and learn along the way. However, this means that you must begin the process early enough to have several right answers from which to choose.

Do Anything Rather than Nothing

Take small steps. If you are putting off studying for a test, set a timer for 10 minutes to reread the first textbook chapter rather than fret about not spending two hours at your desk. You will probably find yourself going past the 10 minutes once you get started and gain momentum. Or, if you are procrastinating about filling out college application forms, start by tackling just one page of one form rather than the entire stack. Small steps are the best way to overcome inertia and gain a sense of accomplishment.

Returning to that essay that is due, begin by writing just one paragraph, any paragraph, even if it's not the introductory paragraph. When you sit down to write, if you know that you need only write that one paragraph, you are less likely to freeze or panic at the thought of producing the entire essay. Who knows? You might just keep writing and have an entire draft before you know it.

Learn to Say No

Especially if you are overscheduled, learn to say a polite but firm "no" to requests on your time or energy that are not necessary and that don't fit with your goals. The world will not come to an end if other people are disappointed with your choices. Your days, your time, and your schedule are ultimately your responsibility, and while it's always good to consider other people's needs as well, be sure not to sacrifice your own needs and peace of mind just to live up to your reputation as someone who "always comes through" or to take on more responsibility than you know you should.

Think about How You Want to Feel in the Future

When the urge to procrastinate creeps up on you, ask yourself how you want to feel later in the day or tomorrow morning or a week from now. If you do your homework today, you can wake up tomorrow feeling rested and ready for the day. On the other hand, if you wait until later tonight, you will have to stay up so late that you will wake up tired and grumpy, or you might even have leftover work to cram in before the school day begins. Doing the errands your dad asked you to do now will mean that you won't have to worry later about his having to remind you or his being upset. In this way, choosing not to procrastinate is something you do for yourself because you want to control how you will feel.

Plan to Procrastinate

Finally, you can use procrastination to your advantage. Especially for people who are natural multi-taskers, "constructive procrastination" can help you to accomplish a lot of work in a short period of time. It works like this: make a list of everything you need to do for a given day or week. Then choose one or two items that you will put off, for now. These should be items that are important but that can wait just a bit longer if need be. Then look at the rest of your list and start doing those items, in any order, as a form of procrastination. Don't allow yourself to do anything that's not on the list. Of course, you still have the one or two remaining items that you put off, but now you have no choice but to finish them. By making procrastination a game, at the end of the day or week, you will have whittled down your to-do list considerably, all in the name of procrastinating!

Mastering Space and Time

Read the following description of how creative people stay in control of their environment and time, from the book *Creativity: Flow and the Psychology of Discovery and Invention* by Mihaly Csikszentmihalyi:

> *Most creative individuals find out early what their best rhythms are for sleeping, eating, and working, and abide by them, even when it is tempting to do otherwise. They wear clothes that are comfortable, they interact only with people they find congenial, they do only things they think are important.… A similar control extends to the structuring of time. Some creative people have extremely tight schedules and can tell you in advance what they will be doing between three and four in the afternoon on a Thursday two months from today. Others are much more relaxed and in fact pride themselves on not know what they will be doing later on today. Again, what matters is not whether one keeps to a strict or to a flexible schedule; what counts is to be master of one's own time.* (p.145)

Think about your own mastery of space and time, and do some freewriting (see page 54) in response to these questions:

- What sleeping rhythm helps you to be most rested, energetic, and creative?
- What eating rhythm helps you to be most rested, energetic, and creative?
- What working or studying rhythm helps you to be most rested, energetic, and creative?
- Do you ever ignore these rhythms for the sake of conformity or peer pressure?
- Do you prefer a strict schedule or a loose schedule?
- If you prefer a strict schedule, do you take the time for yourself to write down that schedule as a way to keep your mind freer for creative thought?
- If you prefer a loose schedule, are you careful not to allow your time to be monopolized by last-minute requests from others or long periods of time that later feel wasted?

○ How often do you feel in control of your time? Most of the time? Sometimes? Never?

○ What is one small change you can make today that will make you feel more in control and lead to more space and time for creativity?

Creativity Websites and Tools

The next time you find yourself looking for something to do other than mindlessly surfing the Web, check out these sites for some creative inspiration:

○ "The Creative Personality," by Mihaly Csikszentmihalyi
www.psychologytoday.com/print/21439

This article from *Psychology Today* is a clear and fascinating discussion of Mihaly Csikszentmihalyi's 10 dimensions of complexity. If the link above doesn't work, go to www.psychologytoday.com and search for "The Creative Personality."

○ Mind-Mapping
www.buzanworld.com/Mind_Maps.htm

Tony Buzan's technique of mind mapping is a visual, nonlinear way to think through, record, and connect information. Many of my college students find it an effective way of taking notes, planning essays, and studying for tests. Visit Tony Buzan's website to learn how to Mind Map and to see several examples.

○ "Seeing the Ordinary as Extraordinary," by Dewitt Jones
www.dewittjones.com/html/everyday.shtml

Dewitt Jones, a *National Geographic* photographer, offers clear and empowering advice for how to see and live life in a more creative way. The article is based on his DVD titled *Everyday Creativity*. Look for the DVD in your local public or university library.

○ Talent Development Resources
http://talentdevelop.com

Douglas Eby's Talent Development Resources website offers information and inspiration to enhance creative expression and personal development in a fun and engaging format.

○ TED Talks: Ideas Worth Spreading
www.ted.com

TED (Technology, Entertainment, Design) Talks is an amazing, free collection of lectures on creativity, invention, the future, and almost any important big idea you can think of by people like Bill Gates, J.J. Abrams, Jeff Bezos, Michelle Obama, and Jane Goodall.

Part III

Becoming a Self-Directed Learner: Teaching Yourself and Learning from Others

Chapter 15

What Is Self-Directed Learning?

Self-directed learning emphasizes your role as an active learner. You are not just a passive receptacle of information who stores data and gives it back when asked. You learn because you choose to learn.

Self-directed learner. Autonomous learner. Autodidact. Unschooler. Life-long learner. All of these terms can refer to the same idea: someone who takes charge of his or her own education.

> *By the time I began my high school coursework, I was very independent and motivated in my studies. My parents gave me a sense of what high school requirements were, and from there I created my own curriculum and schedule. Each week I prepared a calendar that included my goals for each day. If I was able, I would work ahead for the week. If something was not completed, I would move it to the next day, and so on. My parents were always available for any question or problems I was having, but overall, I was completely responsible for my education. I completed my high school requirements in just over two years. ~Kendra, homeschooler*

> *[S]elf-directedness depends on who is in charge—who decides what should be learned, who should learn it, what methods and resources should be used, and how the success of the effort should be measured. To the*

> *extent the learner makes those decisions, the learning is*
> *generally considered to be self-directed.* (Lowry, 1989)

Recent years have seen a great interest in self-directed learning, both as an approach to adult education for lifelong learning and as an aspect of gifted education. Progressive schools and teachers are finding ways to incorporate self-directed learning into classroom education, and several excellent books are published each year for the general public, showing adults how to give themselves the education they wish they'd had.

Do you think of yourself as self-directed? No? You are a self-directed learner whenever you do any of the following:

- ✔ Take the initiative to learn something, whether on your own or with others' help.
- ✔ Pinpoint your learning needs and styles.
- ✔ Set your own learning goals, big or small.
- ✔ Identify and find resources to help you to learn.
- ✔ Use learning strategies that work for you.
- ✔ Evaluate the effectiveness of your learning.

Think about the last time you learned something on your own, not for a class or to fill an outside requirement. Let's suppose you taught yourself a new computer language:

- ✔ You took the initiative. You didn't learn it because someone else told you to.
- ✔ You thought about how you would learn best: by an online tutorial, using a library book, asking someone to help you, taking a class, or through trial and error.
- ✔ You had an idea of how well or how much of the language you wanted to learn and when you wanted to accomplish your goals (note that this can be true even if you didn't write down those goals or a timetable for reaching them).

✔ You identified and chose resources based on how you learn best.

✔ You used learning strategies that work for you, such as immersion learning (spending long periods of time focusing intently on a topic), hands-on learning, intense short bursts of study every day, taking detailed notes as you learn, talking about what you are learning with someone, or some other learning style or method.

✔ Along the way, you evaluated the effectiveness of your learning by adjusting your learning resources and methods based on how well you were learning the material and skills.

As you can see, you are probably more self-directed than you realize. When our learning is self-directed, we learn better and more easily, not to mention with more joy and flow. Of course, no one is self-directed 100% of the time, but the challenge is to include as much self-direction as possible in your education.

Take a look again at the list above of ways that you can be self-directed. Suppose you cannot choose what you study, at least for the time being. You also don't control the main resources that you have to use or how your work is evaluated. What you still might be able to control, however, are the use of outside resources, setting your own learning goals apart from those set by your teacher, determining your own expectations for your grade, and how you organize your time and space for study. Once you are clear about what you can control and what you can't, focus on what you can. Otherwise you might mistakenly think you have no control at all.

For intense learners, self-direction is especially useful. As an intense learner, you—more so than many other people—like to control the pace of your learning, have a strong internal drive to do things your own way, and probably have many broad interests. For these reasons, George Betts created a program for gifted learners called The Autonomous Learner Model. He defines an autonomous learner this way:

> *An autonomous learner is one who solves problems or develops new ideas through a combination of divergent and convergent thinking, and functions with minimal external guidance in selected areas of endeavor.* (2003, p. 38)

The Autonomous Learner Model is a program designed to help gifted students become self-directed learners. One aspect of the model that adapts particularly well both to independent learning and to homeschooling is the fifth and final dimension of the program, called In-Depth Study. In In-Depth Study, you choose an area of passion or high interest, design a project or unit, share it with others, and finally evaluate your own learning. The area you choose to study could be anything from math or history to car engines or comparative religions. If you want to introduce a teacher or parent to Betts's ideas, you can download the article "The Autonomous Learning Model for High School Programming," by George Betts, from the publisher's website: www.alpspublishing.com/alm.html.

Not only is self-directed learning well-suited for gifted learners, but it also helps prepare you for college study and adult learning. Successfully managing college coursework depends heavily on being able to figure out your learning styles, take the initiative to ask for help when you need it, use the resources that work best for you, and evaluate your progress in specific classes and in your overall education. And self-directed learning doesn't stop there. About 70% of adult learning is self-directed, both at home and in the workplace. So self-directed learning isn't just a good technique for middle school and high school; it's good preparation for life.

How Self-Directed Learners Handle Classroom Learning

When you are learning on your own, being self-directed might seem easy. But what about when you are in school? What if a class is too easy? Or too hard? What if a teacher doesn't understand your learning style? What if you are taking a course that you simply don't like?

You won't always have ideal classes, and even superb teachers aren't the best fit for all students. The good news is that self-directed learning gives you tools and perspectives to deal with less-than-perfect situations. The goal isn't to have complete control over every aspect of a class, but to figure out what control you do have and use it.

It is always a good idea to talk to your teacher or parent if you have a problem, but before you do so, think about exactly what isn't working for you. Rather than say that the class or subject is too easy or boring, explain that you already learned the material at a summer science camp. Instead of complaining that you just don't get it, be specific and say that you get stuck on the quadratic formula and could use suggestions on how to learn it better or differently. Or, like Erica, you might simply need some outside motivation:

> *I feel that I am a self-directed and independent learner; do not confuse this with "self-motivated." I definitely still benefit from a swift kick in the rear.* -Erica, university honors student

Adults might surprise you with their receptiveness and ideas, or you might be disappointed. In either case, you have taken the first step. Even if you don't get results from your first conversation, keep up an ongoing dialogue so that your teachers and parents know what parts of your learning are working for you and what parts are not.

Remember the five different intensities? Ask yourself if any of them is affecting your learning. Is something else going on in your life that is triggering emotional intensity and making it hard for you to concentrate? Would you learn the subject better if you could do hands-on tasks in addition to learning from a textbook? If you are having difficulty understanding a work of literature, would it help to listen to it as an audio book after you have read the printed text?

Maybe the problem is mainly one of expectations, in which you or others think that you should have more passion for a subject that you simply aren't very interested in. Similarly, if you decide that getting a B in a course is acceptable rather than an A, you might enjoy the class more, and paradoxically, you may even learn the material better because you can do less stressful cramming and more engaged learning. On the other hand, maybe your expectations for yourself

Avoiding Boredom at All Costs

I'm not that unusual when it comes to my interests. I like reading, computer games, various sports...same old same old. I am one of those weird kids who actually enjoys learning, especially when it comes to foreign languages. I think that's one of my biggest hobbies—the study of language. Languages are extremely fascinating to me. I spend a lot of my free time perfecting my Japanese. I find that I am most happy when I am mastering a skill. I think the very action of testing myself at something and gradually improving the way I do it gives my life meaning. That, or it just keeps me busy! Either way, I find that to be one of the best ways I can improve myself as a human being. Mostly, my long-term plans are avoiding boredom at all costs. -Casey

are too low, preventing your working hard enough for flow to happen.

Regardless of what class you are in, who your teacher is, or what textbooks you are using, there is one thing you can always control: your attitude toward your own work. When you have exhausted other possibilities or while you are waiting for change to be put into place, no one can stop you from choosing to enjoy even the most boring homework, just as no one can stop you from choosing to be miserable about it. Go back to the idea of flow in Chapter 11. What can you do to make the activity more challenging? More interesting? Can you change *how* you complete an assignment? When? Where? Or can you think of a reward to give yourself upon completion that will make the work less tedious?

While you cannot control everything, you can always control something about almost any learning situation. Find it, and go with the flow.

What Do You Want to Know or Do?

But what if you don't know what you want to learn?

Think back to when you were very young. Do you remember never being at a loss for interests? Always asking questions and being surprised every day by how much you wanted to learn and know how to do?

That curiosity and drive to know are still in you. What happens to many teens is that the day-to-day grind of an overscheduled, overstressed life temporarily puts you on autopilot. You have simply had no time to indulge your innate curiosity or practice your inborn skills of self-directed learning. I've even heard busy high school students say that they are afraid to slow down or follow their interests because they fear it would be too hard to go back to their hectic life if they allowed themselves to slow down even a little bit.

If this sounds familiar, here are a few ideas to slow down, rediscover your natural curiosity, and rekindle your passion for learning on your own:

- ✔ Remember what you loved to do as a young child. If you need help remembering, ask your parents or siblings, or look through photo albums or scrapbooks. Do any of these memories tug at your mind or heart again? If at age four you could list 50 different dinosaurs in alphabetical order, perhaps now you would like to revisit that interest, but in a deeper way. You might enjoy going on a dinosaur dig, taking a teen or adult class in paleontology, or volunteering at your local natural history museum. Or if you used to spend hours reading children's stories about dragons and sorcerers but haven't read a book "for fun" in years, get acquainted with the young adult and adult fantasy section of your library.

- ✔ Give yourself what Julia Cameron, author of *The Artist's Way: A Spiritual Path to Greater Creativity*, calls an Artist Date. The Artist Date is an hour or two that you spend with yourself every week recharging your creative juices. You might go to a museum, take a walk in a park, or even go to an arts and crafts store. Browsing in a library is a wonderful Artist Date, especially if you allow yourself at least an hour to scan the shelves, pull down any title that looks interesting, and read only what brings you pleasure.

- ✔ Go to Hoagies' Gifted Page's (Free) Online High School Courses & Curriculum Materials at www.hoagiesgifted.org/online_hs.htm and start browsing. Here you will find terrific resources for everything from screenwriting to Greek, all reviewed by an expert in gifted education.

✔ Get inspired by reading one of these two books for life-long learners: *Peak Learning*, by Ronald Gross, and *What You Need to Read to Know just about Everything: The 25 Best Books for a Self Education and Why*, by Allen L. Scarbrough.

✔ Use a lateral thinking technique, developed by Edward de Bono, called "wishful thinking." Find a time when you can be alone and quiet, and spend several minutes imagining that you have 24 hours when you can do anything you want. Anything. You have no deadlines, no need for sleep. You can go anywhere in the world (or beyond). Your budget is limitless. Try to think of at least 20 things that you would like to do with your ideal day. Write them down. Now look at them and ask yourself which ones give you ideas for things that you can do or learn right now. Often we don't allow our minds to go to our best ideas because we censor them too quickly as being impractical or impossible. The technique of wishful thinking quiets that censor.

✔ Browse Beatrice J. Elyé's book *Teen Success! Ideas to Move Your Mind* and choose a topic such as solitude or mentors or frustration to focus on for the day. *Teen Success!* offers short, accessible chapters about issues that teens face regularly, providing suggestions for how to think about those issues, as well as inspirational quotations to keep you motivated.

If your life is too busy to allow any self-directed learning, you might want to rethink your educational plan, especially if all of your waking hours are spent with the goal—whether your goal or someone else's—of getting into one specific college. No form of secondary schooling, whether the most expensive private high school or the most tailored homeschool, will guarantee that you get into a particular college. Competition for top colleges is fiercer than ever. Even students whose transcripts boast perfect GPAs and SAT scores, dozens of extracurricular activities, and volunteer trips across the globe are not guaranteed a spot at Harvard or Princeton. The question then becomes not how to game the system to secure one of these spots, but whether those spots are as crucial as we think they are.

Of course, there is nothing wrong with wanting to go to a certain tier of universities or even a specific school. I am certainly not saying that the goal of an Ivy League education is a bad one. After all, I married a Princeton graduate. However, as an intense learner, you might feel more pressure than other students to do so because that's just what gifted students do. Be sure that it's also what you want to do before making it the focus of your life.

Michael Winerip, who interviews potential Harvard students, wrote this in his *New York Times* article "Young, Gifted, and Not Getting into Harvard":

> *What kind of kid doesn't get into Harvard? Well, there was the charming boy I interviewed with 1560 SATs. He did cancer research in the summer; played two instruments in three orchestras; and composed his own music. He redid the computer system for his student paper, loved to cook, and was writing his own cookbook. One of his specialties was snapper poached in tea and served with noodle cake.*

If this boy was doing cancer research, playing and composing music, working with computers, and cooking gourmet foods because he loved doing so, the story has a happy ending. His high school years were spent doing what he wanted to do, and he will certainly be able to get a high-quality education at another college or university. If, however, he was doing it all just to get into Harvard, the story is a somewhat tragic one.

Online Schooling

In the past few years, online schooling—also called virtual schooling, cyber learning, distance learning, or e-learning—has gained wide popularity as a way for students to supplement their high school coursework, learn about topics on their own, or even get a high school diploma. The idea began long before the Internet, with correspondence classes. In correspondence classes, learners order books and other materials from a correspondence school, do the work at home, mail it in, get feedback, and be graded or even receive diplomas. Online schooling simply takes this idea to the Internet.

Online schooling can take many forms, but the two main ways to school online are with distance learning programs or virtual schools:

✔ *Distance learning.* Some distance learning classes are not that much different from correspondence classes. The lesson plans, textbooks, and other resources are in hard copy, but you submit lessons and coursework online. Other distance learning classes have online textbooks which you can either print or read at your computer. Distance learning programs might allow you to take one or more classes for high school credit to supplement your homeschooling or classroom schooling, or you can enroll in a full-time distance learning program to get a high school diploma.

✔ *Virtual schools.* Recent years have seen many state-sponsored virtual schools that allow elementary and high school students to learn online at home rather than at school. One difference between these programs and supplemental online courses is that you have less flexibility in choosing your coursework and pacing because you are a public school student rather than a homeschooler. In many states, you can also enroll in private virtual schools as a homeschooler.

For an excellent description of online learning, as well as many specific online learning resources, see Kann and Gillis' *Virtual Schooling: A Guide to Optimizing Your Child's Education.*

Know Your Parents' Non-Negotiables

> *There were times when my parents and I had fights or arguments regarding schoolwork. As I got older, however, this seemed to disappear, as I got more and more motivated to do the work they were telling me to do, not because they were telling me to do it, but because I, in my quest to be an educated young adult, thought it was something I ought to do. ~Josh, age 18*

Whether you go to school or homeschool, you will need to know what aspects of your education are non-negotiable and which are not. Talking with your parents about what their expectations are will prevent many disagreements and misunderstandings down the road. What grades do they want you to get? What coursework do they feel is appropriate? How much time do they expect you to spend on homework? Extracurricular activities? How much do they want to be informed about your day-to-day learning? Which of these areas are the most important to them, and which ones are they more flexible about?

Sometimes parents balk at making a specific list. If this happens, you can try to explain that it will be very useful for you. You might need to start small, with a specific area such as grades. They might say that they just want you to do your best. In that case, you can tell them what *your* expectations are for yourself about grades, and ask for their reaction. This might prompt a more detailed conversation, or they might agree with your expectations, in which case you have your answer.

When you know what parts of your education your parents are most unwavering on, you can make a decision: if you disagree with their expectations, try to come to a compromise, or put it on your list of Parent Non-Negotiables and concentrate instead on the things over which you have more control. For example, your parents might insist on your doing homework each night before you use the computer for socializing. If you decide that trying to change their mind about this isn't worth the hassle, see if you can have your bedtime extended by 15 minutes so that you can have more time to chat online with your friends. Or if your parents have a non-negotiable lights-out time at night, see if they are more flexible on your reading in bed for half an hour with a book light or listening to your MP3 player before falling asleep.

When it comes to disagreements with parents and teachers, use principles of self-directed learning. What can you control? What can't you control? Be clear about what you want and why you want it, but also be prepared with a compromise position if you need it. Finally, sometimes winning a battle isn't nearly as important as how you conduct yourself on the field. If you know that you did your best and acted maturely in presenting your case, rest assured that you scored some points with the adults. They noticed, and you might just have better results next time.

Chapter 16
Homeschooling

First, an important caveat: my goal in this chapter is not to convince you or anyone else to homeschool who doesn't want to. Especially if your parents do not want to homeschool (see page 108), making home education work when it's not a unified, family decision is very difficult and almost always unpleasant. Homeschoolers themselves are often the first to say that it's not the right choice for everyone. Here's how one homeschooler who never attended formal school until college put it:

> *Homeschooling is an excellent way to find your own personality, away from stereotypes and peer pressure, which abound in schools. Homeschooling is not right for everyone, but if school doesn't seem to fit you, then it's always an alternative. And, on the other hand, maybe homeschooling doesn't fit you, and you'd be better off in school. I don't mean to bad-mouth schools by suggesting there's nothing good about them; they just don't fit me, and for me, that's all that matters.*

So if you don't homeschool now or never do, that is just fine with me! You can be a self-directed, creative, and intense learner wherever you learn. That's the whole point of self-directed learning. The information on the following pages might even help assure you that homeschooling is not your best educational option. At the very least, it will help you to understand homeschooling and homeschoolers better.

That said, if you are already homeschooling or seriously considering it, this chapter will reassure you it can be an excellent choice for gifted learners. You will learn reasons that intense learners homeschool, be introduced to different ways to homeschool, and get some help with the decision-making process of whether to homeschool or continue homeschooling for high school. Homeschooling was the best decision our family ever made. I loved every minute of it.

Why Homeschool?

There are as many reasons to homeschool as there are homeschoolers. Homeschooling allows students to be more self-directed, use rather than bury skills of divergent learning, and schedule their time to meet their particular learning needs and family commitments. In addition, intense learners in particular often find that homeschooling allows for specialized study and accommodates their intensities.

Homeschooling Allows for Specialized Study

Do you already know what you want to do with your life, have a special passion, or participate at a high level in the arts or sports? For teens whose intensity is already focused like a laser beam in one area, homeschooling frees up valuable time that you can use to hone your skills and do what you love to do:

> *Homeschooling allowed me to lop off a whole bunch of time each day that I would have spent on schoolwork—time I could use to practice violin. Since I intend to make my living as a violinist eventually, this was rather important, as it allowed me to practice three or four hours a day if I wanted to, something I probably wouldn't have been able to do if I had had school most all day and homework to do for hours when I got home.*
> ~Josh, college freshman at Oberlin Conservatory of Music

Malcolm Gladwell posits, in his best-selling book *Outliers*, that one important difference between those who succeed at what they love and those who don't—perhaps as important as innate ability and talent—is the same way that one gets to Carnegie Hall: practice, practice, practice. He cites a study of young musicians:

> [W]hen the students were around the age of eight, real differences started to emerge. The students who would end up the best in their class began to practice more than everyone else: six hours a week by age nine, eight hours a week by age twelve, sixteen hours a week by age fourteen, and up and up, until by the age of twenty they were practicing—that is, purposefully and single-mindedly playing their instruments with the intent to get better—well over thirty hours a week. (pp. 38-39)

I've known gifted students who take advantage of homeschooling to focus on their swimming, skating, music, writing, art design, and sailing in ways that would be very difficult, if not impossible, in a regular school with its full day of classes, emphasis on involvement in many activities, and homework. At the very least, homeschooling allows for study and practice time, as well as time for sleep! For students like the conservatory freshman above, time to practice for one's vocation is a true gift of homeschooling. Of course, this benefit can be abused if families force their children to work too hard, too long, or for the wrong reasons. However, as long as self-directed learning is emphasized and the area of passion is kept in perspective and balance, homeschooling can be a terrific head start for those who are ready.

Homeschooling Accommodates Intensities

If you are intellectually intense, homeschooling allows you to have the best of both worlds. You can take the time to satisfy your curiosity and your need to know without having to stop to change classes or shut the book before your need to know is sated. At the same time, you can decide when it is worth it to play the game *for you*, at least enough to pass through whatever hoops are necessary to reach your goals, without confusing these hoops for your real passions. When you arrange the hoops and choose to jump through them, they aren't nearly as painful as when you navigate someone else's obstacle course.

Homeschooling is a good fit for the other intensities, too. Learning at home can be a lifesaver for those with psychomotor intensity. You no longer need to sit at a desk for several hours a day. You can move around as you learn. You can take stretch breaks. You can schedule physical exercise in a way that gives you the most energy. If you are sensually intense, you can dress comfortably, more easily manage allergies and other sensitivities, and create a work environment that is aesthetically pleasing. Homeschooling allows for plenty of time to indulge your imaginative intensity with leisure reading, drawing, writing, and daydreaming. Finally, people who are emotionally intense can take advantage of the close relationship that they have with their teacher, who in the case of homeschooling usually happens to be their parent. This relationship can be a fountain of emotional support and make learning a truly family enterprise.

Different Ways to Homeschool

What do you think of when you hear the word "homeschooler"? Some common yet competing stereotypes of homeschoolers are that they sleep until noon and study in their pajamas, they spend all day filling out workbooks at a kitchen table, or they sit blurry-eyed at a computer and lack real-life friends.

Many who are unfamiliar with homeschooling assume that homeschoolers learn in a way that is pretty similar to classroom learning. It is "school at home," in which homeschooled kids use textbooks similar to those used in regular school, follow a schedule of classes for different subject areas, and stick to curriculum based on grade levels. Their parents assume the role of teacher, giving grades and setting a schedule, just as classroom teachers do. In this model, the student is a passive vessel filled by the teacher—in this case, a parent.

The reality is that very few homeschoolers actually learn this way, at least not all of the time. After all, why not just go to school instead?

For some new homeschoolers, doing at least a little "school at home" is a familiar and even good way to begin. However, most homeschoolers eventually move toward more self-directed learning and patchwork learning, even if they use a more traditional classroom approach for specific subjects such as math or foreign language.

Of course, if you already learn at home or know other homeschoolers, you know that they are as diverse in the ways in which they learn as anyone else—more so, in fact, because homeschoolers have options that are unavailable to students in the classroom.

How you homeschool depends on many factors, some of which are these:

- ✔ Your family's attitude toward and philosophy of education
- ✔ How you prefer to learn and how you learn best
- ✔ Your family's budget
- ✔ What fits with your family's schedule and living space
- ✔ Your own educational and life goals
- ✔ Your state homeschooling laws

The last item is important, because as a self-directed learner, you should be familiar with your state laws about home education. Don't leave it up to your parents! If you know exactly what you need to do in your state—and what you don't—you have a better chance of working with your parents to create a homeschool plan that works for everyone. To learn more about the homeschooling regulations where you live, visit the A to Z Home's Cool Homeschooling website at http://homeschooling.gomilpitas.com/regional/Region.htm.

With these factors in mind, let's look briefly at a few of the most common ways to homeschool. If you or your parents want more information about homeschooling philosophy and methods, check out my book *Creative Home Schooling: A Resource Guide for Smart Families*.

Unschooling

According to Mary Griffith, author of *The Unschooling Handbook*, unschooling is "learning what one wants, when one wants, where one wants, for one's own reasons" (p. 3). Unschooling advocate Grace Llewellyn writes in *Freedom Challenge: African American*

Homeschoolers, "I often use the term 'unschooling.' 'Homeschooling' can sound like doing *school* at *home*, while the kind of homeschooling that excites me does not resemble school and often takes place as much out in the world—museums, workplaces, riverbanks—as in the home" (p. 11).

I find that unschooling is often misunderstood. At its best, unschooling is self-directed learning 24/7 with a lot of collaboration between learner and adult. It's not "un-education." It's simply getting an education without the artificial trappings of classroom habits and schedules. For unschooling to work well, both you and your parents need to be committed to the belief that you will learn what you want and need to know, when you want and need to know it, by following your interests, asking your own questions, asking for help when you need it, finding and using resources, and setting your own goals.

Unschooling works particularly well for intense learners who are more concerned with the quality of their education than with having an impressive résumé. Instead of making every learning decision with the goal of college applications, you make decisions with the goal of being well-educated. Getting into a specific college may or may not be a part of that process, but for you, that's not the only goal.

Patchwork Homeschooling

Many homeschoolers put together a patchwork of approaches and resources that varies from child to child, subject to subject, and year to year. You might unschool for some subjects, such as literature and history, do a mostly school at home approach for math, and take online courses for science. The next year, you might do something entirely different. Patchwork homeschooling—doing whatever works—allows for a truly individualized education, and it is a very popular homeschooling option. To work well, it also requires creativity and flexible planning.

Part-Time Homeschooling

Depending on your state laws and school district policy, you might be able to attend school part time and homeschool part time.

Some districts allow homeschooled students to take core classes such as math or English, while other districts limit the options to extra-curriculars, such as music or art. Check with both your state and your local school district to see what options are available to you.

Homeschooling while in School

Finally, even if you do not plan to homeschool, you can still think of yourself as homeschooling. If your regular classes are not challenging enough or don't seem relevant to you, use your free time and summers to give yourself the education you need and want, and think of school as your extracurricular time. By taking charge of your own education and learning more about yourself as a learner, you can also find ways to make those classroom hours more interesting and engaging.

But What about College? (Or, Will Homeschooling Ruin My Chances for Success?)

I was always amazed when people asked me how our son would get into college as a homeschooler. It was never something we worried about. While it is true that maybe 10 years ago homeschoolers had difficulty showing colleges and universities that their education was equal to (and sometimes better than) those of their class-room-schooled peers, today the vast majority of colleges and universities, from small community colleges to the Ivies, have application procedures for homeschoolers. According to Cafi Cohen, author of *Homeschoolers' College Admissions Handbook*, 95% of all colleges and universities are open to homeschoolers. For a detailed list of colleges that admit homeschoolers, see Karl Bunday's website Learn in Freedom! at http://learninfreedom.org.

When You (or Your Parents) Don't Want to Homeschool

What if you want to homeschool, but your parents don't? Or your parents want to homeschool, but you would rather not? Is there a compromise? Let's look at each situation and consider your best options.

You Say Yes, They Say No

First, give some thought to exactly why you want to learn at home. Write down your reasons so that you can remember them and explain them clearly. Look again at the different ways to home-school, and decide which approaches would work well for you. Then, find a time to talk to your parents honestly about how you feel. Ask them why they don't want to try homeschooling. Listen closely to their answers.

They might be afraid that homeschooling will be too much work for them. They might worry that leaving school would hurt your chances at college or a career. Or they might be concerned that your relationship with them would suffer if you are around home so much.

The problem could also be a logistical one. They might wonder how homeschooling could possibly fit into an already hectic family schedule. Or, if you are going to public school and thus have few educational expenses, they might feel that the cost of homeschooling is beyond your family budget.

All of these are valid concerns. Be prepared to state your case and offer creative solutions, but also be prepared for the fact that your parents may not change their minds. This is a decision that you will need to accept. Homeschooling is a big commitment, and one that needs to be made with everyone on board. If you really want to learn at home, however, don't give up. Wait a few weeks and ask again. In the meantime, show your parents with your actions that you have the self-discipline and motivation to make homeschooling work.

They Say Yes, You Say No

You might be reading this book reluctantly because one or both of your parents think that you should homeschool, or they think that you should take more responsibility for your homeschooling. If you are reluctant to homeschool or just plain don't want to, again, think about, write down, and present your reasons. If your parents are not convinced, ask them if you can homeschool for a trial period—a semester is a good length, or maybe even a year. Depending on the flexibility of your school, you might even be able to work at home for as little as a month or so, and then reevaluate. Another option is to ask you parents if you can homeschool for a summer as a trial period.

See how it goes. I know many students who homeschool for one or two years, and they always learn valuable things about themselves in the process, even if they decide that long-term homeschooling is not for them. As Julio, age 13, advises, "Stick with it, even if it doesn't seem to work right away. It's tough to get going right away if you've just started. Give it a while."

Intense Learners Discuss Homeschooling

I'd say that throughout my high school years, I both became more organized and also more confident in my ability to schedule my time. Finding the balance between structure and freedom was hardest early on. Taking distance learning high school courses, and later in-person college courses, was very helpful, as I could follow a predetermined set of goals and yet still within that format learn what was the best way for me to achieve them. ~College classics major

Homeschooling for high school was empowering, and it gave me a sense of independence and responsibility that has remained with me through my college education. It takes a lot of initiative and motivation, but it's absolutely worth it. I think many teenagers might be concerned about missing out on the social aspects of school, but between extracurricular activities, volunteering, and working, it's really not an issue. In short, I think if you're unhappy in a traditional learning environment, homeschooling is definitely worth a try.

I also think that homeschooling is possibly more beneficial to the gifted learner than to a more average student because a gifted learner is more likely to be bored or to struggle in a traditional setting. Homeschooling allows parents and their children to work together in order to create a curriculum and environment that fits the learning style and educational needs of the children (or young adults). ~College biological sciences and chemistry major

I think the main advantages of homeschooling were more freedom, a more nurturing learning environment, and a curriculum better adapted to my needs. Since it is the parents doing the schooling, not a rigid, state-based system, there is a lot more flexibility. ~College exchange student in Japan

Homeschooling provided me with a stealth-learning training ground for self-advocacy; from capricious roommates to recalcitrant teaching assistants, self-advocacy is a must-have for college! Additionally, by taking classes at the community college, I have the confidence to call a professor or department I'm unfamiliar with to discuss course offerings and departmental events, and to campaign for admittance to closed/ restricted classes.

I really feel that homeschooling during the elementary years was a positive experience; unlike my classmates, I entered high school and college without feeling "burned out" on learning and the school system. ~College honors student, age 16

Chapter 17

College and Beyond: Non-Traditional Paths

The traditional continuous path from four years of high school to college—especially for bright students—is almost unquestioned in our society today. The question that you hear is probably rarely *if* or even *when* you will go to college; the question is *where*.

Of course, there is nothing wrong with going straight from high school to college. In fact, doing so has some clear advantages. If you are interested in a subject such as math or science that relies on a progression of detailed knowledge, you do not lose momentum. You might find it easier to keep the schedule of standardized testing and college applications in your senior year, when others your age are doing the same. Your family might be more ready and willing to support you financially when you are 18 rather than 25. And you will have the experience of being in a class with others who are close to your age and who have the shared experience of having just completed high school.

That said, don't immediately dismiss other options without giving them at least some thought. If you do decide to take the more traditional route, you will then be making a fully informed decision rather than just going to college at age 18 because…well, that's what everyone does, right?

Not necessarily.

Here are a few non-traditional options for life after high school that you might want to consider.

Starting College in High School

Many high school students are ready for college work before age 18. Sometimes AP classes are challenging enough to fit this need, but you can also look into taking one or more college courses while in high school, as this student did:

> I started taking college classes when I was 15. This was mostly because I wanted to study Japanese, and there was almost no other means to do so outside of college. I enrolled as a "special high school student" and took their five-credit basic Japanese course. Compared to the part-time high school classes I had taken previously, I found college to be much more desirable. There was much more focus on the material at hand, and I found the quickened pace of the class to be much better than the slow tedium of high school.

Some schools have a dual enrollment program that allows you to take classes either during the school day or at night. Your high school might even cover the costs of the classes. You can also look into taking online college courses. If you homeschool, check if your state or school district's dual enrollment policy applies to homeschoolers, or look into enrolling as a part-time, non-degree student at a community college or local university. Another option is to audit a college class or two before you take one for a grade.

Early College

Instead of taking part-time college classes in high school, you can also consider enrolling early in college full time before age 18. Depending on where you live, you might be able to do this at a local college so that you can live at home. Other teens travel to early college programs designed specifically for young students. There are several early college programs for gifted learners. For more information, see

Considering the Options: A Guidebook for Investigating Early College Entrance (student version), by Nancy M. Robinson, available as a free download from the Davidson Institute for Talent Development at www.davidsongifted.org.

Even for the brightest students, however, early college is not always the best answer. A 19-year-old college senior offers this advice:

> I think you should make the decision to go to college early carefully. If you decide to go, I suggest easing into it. Remember that you are more free at this point in your life than you'll ever be, and that full-time college is a full-time job (and then some!). Finishing the high school requirements early is a great accomplishment, and it gives you even more opportunities to explore interests. Still, if you feel that you have gotten everything possible out of your education, then it is time to move forward. This was the case for me, and college seemed to be the natural next step.

Two-Year Colleges, Technical Schools, and Associate Degrees

You don't need me to tell you that college is expensive. According to the College Board (2009), average yearly expenses at a private, four-year university were about $39,000 in 2009-10. Students who went to a public, four-year university paid $31,000 if they came from out of state, and a little over $19,000 if they were in-state residents. By contrast, the average yearly cost of a two-year, public associate degree was $14,000. Students who commuted to these two-year colleges rather than lived on campus paid just under $7,000.

A student I once had in a technical writing course wrote a paper about the advantages of getting an associate degree before applying to a four-year program. This was the path he had followed, and he was one of the brightest students I've ever taught. Going to a two-year program not only allowed him to save money while getting some entry-level courses out of the way, he also was able to "try out" classes in his chosen major before committing to double-digit tuition figures. Because he had done his homework, he knew ahead of time which courses would transfer to the four-year school of his choice, and he was able to transfer in as a second semester sophomore.

I also know many homeschooled students who have gone to a two-year state school before transferring to one of the state system's four-year schools. This option offers many advantages, especially for students who are considering starting college a year or two early. If the college is close enough, you can live at home, giving you one less transition to deal with as you get used to a college schedule. Showing that you can do well in college classrooms can make it easier to convince a larger, four-year college that you are prepared for the rigors of full-time, residential college life. If you are interested in this kind of dual enrollment (see page 112), you might be able to start taking classes part time at a two-year or technical college and still be considered a high school student. Also, some states with very selective main campuses have a guarantee transfer program for students who do well enough in a satellite, two-year school.

The quality of teachers at all colleges can range from poor to outstanding. However, instructors at two-year schools tend to be extremely dedicated to their teaching. They do not have the publishing requirements of university professors, so their focus is on the classroom and the students. The important thing to remember is that, as my father-in-law used to say, you take your brain with you wherever you go. As a self-directed learner, you will maximize your education wherever you are, and there is nothing wrong with taking your time, saving some money, and going to a two-year program after high school, especially if you are unsure of your major, if you are financially strapped, or if you want to live at home for a couple of years.

Taking a Year (or More) Off

Finally, if you know you want to go to college but feel rushed to decide where to go, or if you simply don't feel ready to make the transition right after high school, consider taking one or more years off before continuing your classroom education. Many colleges and universities allow you to defer your enrollment for a year after you have been accepted. You can use the year to work, study, travel—

almost anything your budget allows. You can even consider yourself a college homeschooler, using your self-directed learning to explore topics and ideas at a college level on your own. If you are interested in travel, a book that will inspire you is *The New Global Student: Skip the SAT, Save Thousands on Tuition, and Get a Truly International Education*, by Maya Frost.

In all of these non-traditional options, the important thing to remember is that they are available to you as an intense, gifted learner. Don't buy into the myth that being gifted limits your choices rather than expands them. Waiting to go to college, going to a local college, or even not going to college at all are viable options and do not make you less smart, regardless of what anyone else says. If you don't believe me, do an Internet search for "successful people who didn't go to college" or "successful people who didn't go to Ivy League colleges." As acclaimed science fiction author Ray Bradbury said, "I never went to college. I went to the library."

A Conclusion in which Nothing Is Concluded: Weaving Your Own Education Tapestry

This may be the final segment of this book, but for you, it's just the beginning. As I wrote in the introduction, my hope is that after reading this book, you will never view your education the same way again. Wherever you go to school or whatever teachers or classmates you have, you now have a better understanding of yourself as an intense, creative, and self-directed learner. You can control your own thoughts. You know that you are able to evaluate your learning environment, recognize what you can't change, and make the most of what you can. Because you are a life-long learner, you will continue this process of learning with intensity long after you walk down the graduation aisle.

I like to think of life-long education as a beautiful tapestry that we weave day by day, year by year. The warp threads—the ones that form the tension of your "canvas" and the invisible background of your design—are your learning environment, teachers, parents, classroom, and everything that is outside of you. Some of these threads you can reposition, remove, or add; others you cannot.

The weft threads—the ones that you pass back and forth through the warp threads to form your design—are strands of intensity, creativity, and self-directed learning. They all work together to strengthen your education and form a unique, beautiful life story.

You weave your tapestry one day at a time, working according to a plan and, at the same time, making design changes as necessary along the way. Sometimes you even weave freeform for a while, just to see what happens. Some days you weave quickly, other days with more leisure. But you never stop weaving.

Before I go, I will leave you with seven reminders of what you have learned and some suggestions for making the most of your intensity, creativity, and self-direction as you weave your new tapestry.

Habits of Mind for Intense Learners

1. Be aware of the negative self-talk that you use to refer to your own intensities, and begin to talk to yourself as you would to a good friend. Here are some examples:

Instead of…	Think of yourself as…
Too intense	Wonderfully intense
Geeky	Super smart
Hyper	Energetic
Fidgety	Thinking with my body
Too sensitive	In tune with my senses and environment
Prissy	Appreciative of cleanliness and neatness
Distracted	Imaginative
Too emotional	Emotionally rich and complex
Not fitting in	Just where I should be
No one likes me	I do have friends
Life isn't fair	I have more opportunities than I realized

2. Look for signs of intensity in the people around you: parents, siblings, friends, teachers. Do this especially when they have habitual traits and behaviors that make you a little crazy.

3. Remember that not everyone has the same intensities you do. They won't necessarily understand your reactions or feelings, and you won't fully understand theirs. There is nothing wrong with this. Tolerance of and respect for differences is the answer.

4. Don't fall for the temptation to use intensities as an excuse for rude or thoughtless words or actions. It's one thing to try to educate your parents about how you study better when the house is quiet. It's quite another to insist on total silence by sulking or yelling or dictating.

5. Remember to give yourself a planning time every once in a while—at least once a month—when you ask yourself how things are going and if you need to adjust your goals or plan new intermediate steps.

6. Every day, be sure to learn at least one thing just for you, even if only for a few minutes. Count every day in which you learn something new as a good day.

7. Congratulate yourself for successes along the way, especially the ones that no one else sees.

References

Adderholdt, M., & Goldberg, J. (1999). *Perfectionism: What's bad about being too good?* (Rev. ed.). Minneapolis, MN: Free Spirit.

Aron, E. N. (1999). *The highly sensitive person: How to thrive when the world overwhelms you.* Bridgewater, NJ: Replica Books.

Betts, G. T. (2003, Fall/Winter). The autonomous learning model for high school programming. *Gifted Education Communicator: A Journal for Educators and Parents,* 38-41, 60-61.

Cameron, J. (2002). *The artist's way: A spiritual path to greater creativity.* Kirkwood, NY: Putnam.

Cohen, C. (2002). *Homeschoolers' college admissions handbook.* New York: Crown/Three Rivers Press.

College Board. (2009, October). *Trends in student pricing 2009* (Trends in Higher Education Series). Washington, DC: Author. (Available online at www.trends-collegeboard.com/college_pricing/pdf/2009_Trends_College_Pricing.pdf.)

Crist. J. J. (2007). *Mad: How to deal with your anger and get respect.* Minneapolis, MN: Free Spirit.

Csikszentmihalyi, M. (1997). *Creativity: Flow and the psychology of discovery and invention.* New York: Harper Perennial.

Csikszentmihalyi, M. (1998). *Finding flow: The psychology of engagement with everyday life.* New York: Basic Books.

Csikszentmihalyi, M. (2008). *Flow: The psychology of optimal experience.* New York: Harper Perennial.

Csikszentmihalyi, M., Rathunde, K., & Whalen, S. (1996). *Talented teenagers: The roots of success and failure.* New York: Cambridge University Press.

Daniels, S. J., & Piechowski, M. M. (Eds.). (2008). *Living with intensity: Understanding the sensitivity, excitability, and emotional development of gifted children, adolescents, and adults.* Scottsdale, AZ: Great Potential Press.

Elbow, P. (1973). *Writing without teachers.* Oxford, MA: Oxford University Press.

Elyé, B. J. (2007). *Teen success! Ideas to move your mind* (2nd ed.). Scottsdale, AZ: Great Potential Press.

Frost, M. (2009). *The new global student: Skip the SAT, save thousands on tuition, and get a truly international education.* New York: Crown/Three Rivers Press.

Gladwell, M. (2008). *Outliers: The story of success.* New York: Little, Brown.

Griffith, M. (1998). *The unschooling handbook.* New York: Crown/Three Rivers Press.

Gross, R. (1999). *Peak learning.* New York: Penguin/Tarcher.

Hipp, E. (2008). *Fighting invisible tigers: Stress management for teens* (3rd ed.). Minneapolis, MN: Free Spirit.

Jacobsen, M. E. (2000). *The gifted adult: A revolutionary guide for liberating everyday genius.* New York: Ballantine Books.

Johnson, S. (1998). *Who moved my cheese? An amazing way to deal with change in your work and in your life.* New York: Putnam.

Johnson, S. (2002). *Who moved my cheese? for teens.* New York: Putnam.

Kann, E., & Gillis, L. (2009). *Virtual schooling: A guide to optimizing your child's education.* New York: Palgrave Macmillan.

Laney, M. O. (2002). *The introvert advantage: How to thrive in an extrovert world.* New York: Workman.

Lewis, B. A. (1998). *The teen guide to social action.* Minneapolis, MN: Free Spirit.

Llewellyn, G. (1996). *Freedom challenge: African American homeschoolers.* Eugene, OR: Lowry House.

Lowry, C. M. (1989). *Supporting and facilitating self-directed learning* (ERIC Digest #93). Columbus, OH: ERIC Clearinghouse on Adult Career and Vocational Education. (Available online at www.ericdigests.org/pre-9213/self.htm.)

Piechowski, M. M. (2006). *"Mellow out," they say. If I only could: Intensities and sensitivities of the young and bright.* Madison, WI: Yunasa Books.

Piirto, J. (2004). *Understanding creativity.* Scottsdale, AZ: Great Potential Press.

Rivero, L. (2002). *Creative home schooling: A practical guide for smart families.* Scottsdale, AZ: Great Potential Press.

Robinson, K. (2009). *The element: How finding your passion changes everything.* New York: Viking.

Robinson, N. M. (2005). *Considering the options: A guidebook for investigating early college entrance* (student version). Retrieved December 21, 2009, from http://print.ditd.org/young_scholars/Guidebooks/Davidson_Guidebook_EarlyCollege_Students.pdf

Scarbrough, A. L. (2002). *What you need to read to know just about everything: The 25 best books for a self education and why.* San Jose, CA: Writers Club Press.

Winerip, M. (2007, April 29). Young, gifted, and not getting into Harvard. *New York Times.* Retrieved December 20, 2009, from www.nytimes.com/2007/04/29/nyregion/nyregionspecial2/29Rparenting.html

Index

resources for, 105
stereotypes of, 104
unschooling as, 105-6
while in school, 107, 112
Hughes, Joseph, 27

imaginational intensity, 19, 37-9,
 45, 104
 forms and expressions of, 21-2
 learning and, 38
 relationships and, 38-9
inertia, overcoming, 60-1, 82
intellectual intensity, 19, 23-8, 45,
 103
 forms and expressions of, 20-1
 learning and, 24-6
 programs for those with, 28
 relationships and, 26-7
intensity/intensities, 19-20, 46, 64,
 91, 93, 118-19
 forms and expressions of, 20-2
 giftedness and, 12, 19
 homeschooling and, 102-4
 in parents, 45-6
 See also emotional intensity;
  imaginational intensity;
  intellectual intensity;
  psychomotor intensity;
  sensual intensity
Interlochen Arts Camp, 39
introversion, 55-7
Introvert Advantage, The, 46

Jacobsen, Mary-Elaine, 46, 68, 76
James, William, 75
Johns Hopkins Center for Talented
 Youth, 28
Johnson, Shawn, 81
Johnson, Spencer, 51

Jones, Dewitt, 82, 85

King, Jr., Martin Luther, 81

labels, use of, 12
Laney, Marti Olsen, 46
lateral thinking, 51, 96
laziness, redefining, 60-1
*Learning Outside the Lines: Two
 Ivy League Students with
 Learning Disabilities and
 ADHD Give You the Tools*, 32
learning styles, 57-8, 92
Lenney, Dinah, 39
Lewis, Barbara A., 38
Living with Intensity, 20, 38, 46
Llewellyn, Grace, 105

*Mad: How to Deal with Your
 Anger and Get Respect*, 40
Manifesto, E. Paul Torrance's,
 61-2
*"Mellow Out," They Say. If I
 Only Could*, 20, 40
Mooney, Jonathan, 32
Mucklow, Nancy, 36

New Global Student, The, 115
Northwestern University Center
 for Talent Development, 27-8

online schooling, 97-8
organization and scheduling,
 habits of, 70-1
Outliers, 103
overexcitabilities, 19

About the Author

Lisa Rivero lives in Milwaukee, Wisconsin, where she is a writer, teacher, speaker, and parent. She has taught and mentored teens at the middle school, high school, and college levels, and she always enjoys helping young people to discover, appreciate, and use their creativity, drive, passion, and love of learning. She currently teaches at the Milwaukee School of Engineering, and she is a board member of SENG (Supporting Emotional Needs of the Gifted), a national nonprofit organization.

Lisa's articles have appeared in several national publications, among which are *Parenting for High Potential*, *Duke Gifted Letter*, *Roeper Review*, and *Understanding Our Gifted*. Her other books include the award-winning *Creative Home Schooling: A Resource Guide for Smart Families* (2003 Glyph Best Education Book Award); *Gifted Education at Home: A Case for Self-Directed Homeschooling*; *The Homeschooling Option: How to Decide When It Is Right for Your Family*; and *A Parent's Guide to Gifted Teens: Living with Intense and Creative Adolescents*. She speaks at state and national conferences on issues of giftedness, homeschooling, and creativity.